Simone de Beauvoir and the Colonial Experience

Simone de Beauvoir and the Colonial Experience

Freedom, Violence, and Identity

Nathalie Nya

LEXINGTON BOOKS

Lanham • Boulder • New York • London

Published by Lexington Books
An imprint of The Rowman & Littlefield Publishing Group, Inc.
4501 Forbes Boulevard, Suite 200, Lanham, Maryland 20706
www.rowman.com

6 Tinworth Street, London SE11 5AL, United Kingdom

British Library Cataloguing in Publication Information Available

Library of Congress Cataloging-in-Publication Data Available

ISBN 978-1-4985-5809-9 (cloth : alk. paper)
ISBN 978-1-4985-5810-5 (electronic)

♾™ The paper used in this publication meets the minimum requirements of American National Standard for Information Sciences—Permanence of Paper for Printed Library Materials, ANSI/NISO Z39.48-1992.

Printed in the United States of America

To my mother and father, Veronique and John Semple

Contents

Preface

This project's primary aim is to interpret the philosophy of Simone de Beauvoir and her intellectual trajectory through the perspective of French colonial history. I consider Beauvoir through this lens not only to critique her position as a *colonizer woman* or *colon*, but also as a means of situating her in one of France's most vexing and fraught historical moments. Throughout this book, I refer to Beauvoir as a *colonizer woman* or *colon*, in the French, in order to emphasize the weight of French colonialism on Beauvoir's identity as a white French woman and not to negativize her role in the French imperialism. Indeed, I claim that while the French republic was systematizing colonialism, all of its white citizens were *colons,* whereas natives from France's colonies were the *colonized.* Referring to Beauvoir as a colonizer emphasizes the subjective and interpersonal dialectic of colonialism, and the political dynamic between the colonized and the colonizer. In *Freedom, Violence, and Identity*, I present a gendered and female perspective of French colonialism, training particular focus on the period between 1946 and 1962, during which events incited French intellectuals such as Jean-Paul Sartre and Franz Fanon to rally against the political system; and, how their support fostered public opinions that brought about an end to French colonialism. However, although I seek to explicate French colonialism in terms of complex issues of gender and sex, I argue that it is through the work of Beauvoir as a colonizer woman that I am able to develop this feminist perspective of French colonialism in the philosophical tradition. This book adheres to a reading of Beauvoir as foremost an intellectual woman. To this end, I posit and maintain she reflected upon the legacy of French colonialism as an author and her nation-bound status as a colonizer serve an understanding of her relationship with women such as the alliance she created with Gisele Halimi and Djamila Boupacha.

As I contend in these pages, Beauvoir's colonial reflections can help us to better gauge how women—White, Asian, Arab, Caribbean, Latina, mixed race, and Black—decipher the crimes and injustices of French colonialism. Closely reading Beauvoir's work fleshes out the reflections of women on colonial themes, such as gendered and racialized topics concerning *freedom, violence,* and *identity*, pointing to the possibility of women speaking as interlocutors of, and participants in, the dialectic of colonialism, the exchange between the colonized and the colonizer. As such, the story of French colonialism gains subjective and interpersonal freight, in turn, allowing women to serve as both active and passive participant-founders of colonialism.

The first stirrings of this project were in 2010 when I was a graduate student at Penn State University in search of a dissertation topic that would appeal to my interest in French philosophy, critical race philosophy, and feminism. Raised in an interracial family of White-American, Cameroonian, and French origins, I was studying these topics in the context of the education system in the United States and searching for parts of my own history. In the late 1990s to the early 2000s, I was introduced to philosophical analyses on French colonialism, not colonialism in general (as I believe that not all forms of European colonialism were the same; for example, British colonialism was not identical to French colonialism or to Spanish colonialism), through the works of Fanon, Sartre, Aimé Césaire, Albert Camus, Albert Memmi, and Leopold Senghor. For better or worse, these French intellectuals gave a voice to the oppressed—to people with a marginalized status. But as a student of third-wave feminism with an interest in the intersectionalites of race, class, sex, and gender, I was disappointed by the dearth of any genuine representation of women—Asian, Arab, Caribbean, Latina, Black, mixed race, or White, in the thoughts of these male colonial intellectuals. I was not only looking for what they thought about representations of women in the work of these male intellectuals, but also for female authors and/or philosophers who would articulate the struggle of the colonial consciousness in the first-person or from a personal narrative. So, I found Mayotte Capecia, Suzanne Césaire, Paulette Nardal, and, in the end, Simone de Beauvoir. Capecia, Césaire, and Nardal were all French Martinican female authors and Beauvoir, of course, was French. They all provided different female perspectives on the intellectual history of French colonialism.

In 2010, the work of Mayotte Capecia already interested me and, by then, I had written and published an article on Fanon and Mayotte Capecia in *The Caribbean Journal of Philosophy*. Then I turned to the work of Tracy Sharpley-Whiting, a feminist postcolonial scholar, to gain a deeper understanding of Suzanne Césaire and Paulette Nardal. I reviewed and studied their work because of their importance to the development of the Black female perspective within French colonial cultural studies of the twentieth century.

After 2010, it was out of sheer luck that I was able to find even scant scholar-ship on Simone de Beauvoir and her thoughts on colonialism. Like Mayotte Capecia's, the views of Beauvoir on colonialism immediately captured my attention. In *The Ethics* of *Ambiguity*, she talks about the *serious* mood upheld by colonial officers who tortured the population with excessive labor; in one of her memoirs, *Force of Circumstance*, she addresses the Algerian war and its effect on the humanity of the French. In my dissertation, I focus on the work of not only Beauvoir but also Sartre and Fanon, so as to gain a broader area of specialization in twentieth-century French philosophy. While I was in the process of completing and defending my dissertation in 2014, I decided I would like to write my first book on Simone de Beauvoir because, in the field of philosophy, very little work focuses on the French colonial experience and its effects on women—*written from the female perspective*. At that point, in 2016, I became a postdoctoral fellow in the Philosophy Depart-ment at John Carroll University, and this book project began.

Acknowledgments

I am very much indebted to all those friends and colleagues who gave me feedback including Mariana Ortega, Michael Eng, Tom Hanaurt, Shannon Sullivan, and Laura Hengehold. I especially want to acknowledge my family and close friends who have been supportive of my journey as a philosopher including John, Veronique and Jordan Semple, K. Vera Brink, Darwin Bond-Graham, Ryan Beck, Joshua Kurdys, Illeana Sadin, and my dear friend P.

Introduction

In *Unfinished Projects* (2010), Paige Arthur[1] discusses the trajectory of Sartre's thinking throughout the post–World War II political movements that led to the end of colonialism in both colonial and metropolitan France. Arthur argues that Sartre opposed French colonialism in all regions of France, including Algeria, Vietnam, and the sub-Saharan African countries. In her analysis, Arthur aims to emphasize the role of the intellectual in the decolonization process—the writings, the press reviews and conferences, and the organizations formed and led by intellectuals like Sartre. Where Arthur addresses the relationship between the role of the philosopher and de/colonization, my project on Beauvoir relates to hers. The difference in my analysis—and what I add to the discussion of the relationship between the role of the philosopher and the system of colonialism—is that I attempt to construct "the philosopher" as a female figure who can easily embody the thoughts of Beauvoir and who assumes the premise that the issues with colonialism are not just a race problem but a gender and sexual problem as well. My project includes Beauvoir in comparative studies of gender, racial, and colonial oppression in the writings of Sartre and Fanon. I grant strategic significance to scholarship on Fanon (and not just Sartre) because he is a key figure in postcolonial philosophy; even on questions pertaining to feminist issues, such as sex and gender, his contributions must not be overlooked.

This book's chief aim is to perform readings of Beauvoir's body of work in terms of the historical reality of French colonial rule. As such, I examine Beauvoir's essays and memoirs, such as *The Second Sex*, *The Ethics of Ambiguity*, and *Force of Circumstance*, in the context of French colonialism. De Beauvoir's novel *The Mandarins*, published in 1954, vaguely refers to aspects of life in the French and Portuguese colonies—which I find to be based on some gross generalization about the French and Portuguese systems of colonialism and do not reflect the complexity with which she addresses European colonialism in her nonfictional texts. For this reason, I do not focus on this fictional text because I want to account in this book, on the differences between the fictional work and nonfictional work under which Beauvoir writes about the question of colonialism. Although some have argued that *The Mandarins* has some autobiographical content, the goal of this project is to be as more factual about the intellectual history of French colonialism during its end period, with particular attention from 1946 to 1962. This period, which marks the period after World War II, was not just a period in which the process of decolonialization was the focus of French intellectuals' writing and public speeches, the establishment of the fourth and fifth Republic was also the concerns of French intellectuals. The Existentialists, such as Sartre, wrote about this especially in relationship to the elections and presidencies of Vincent Auriol (1947–1954), Rene Coty (1954–1959), and General Charles de Gaulle (1959–1969). However, the establishment of the fourth and fifth Republic was congruent with decolonization in France. Sartre's analysis and public speeches on the relation of the fourth and fifth Republic to colonialism has been written about by contemporary philosophers. Here, I hope to show this in the writings of Beauvoir especially on views on the Women Suffrage in France and her involvement with Djamila Boupacha case. Thus, I want to note here that whenever I mention the term, "French government" or "French administration," in relation to the philosophy of Beauvoir, I am speaking of the fourth and fifth Republic, representing the administrative polities of France primarily influenced by the elections and presidencies of Vincent Auriol, Rene Coty, and General Charles de Gaulle.

I place critical emphasis on Beauvoir's essays and nonfiction writing. Beauvoir's comments on European colonialism in *The Mandarins* only appear in passing—on about 4 out of 600 pages—and thus by no means form a major theme in the development of her narrative. I only mention *The Mandarins* here in order to encourage the reader to think all of the texts Beauvoir wrote during the period under discussion are, to some degree, colonial texts. Between the real and fictitious in this historical moment, colonialism as a political system played a symbolic role in Beauvoir's intellectual trajectory and *oeuvre*. Like her fiction work that tends to deal with complicated love affairs, Beauvoir's nonfiction expounds upon her complicated relations with the idea of French colonialism.

Despite her oppositional stance to French colonialism, Beauvoir was, nevertheless, a *colon*. As such, she demonstrates a thinker's ability to rebel against the very racial position she embodies, in part because she criticized her nation's political order, and by extension, her own place of citizenship. As Sartre expresses in 1948 in "Black Orpheus," his introduction to *An Anthology of the New Negro and Malagasy Poetry in French* (Anthologie de la nouvelle poésie nègre et malgache de langue française) by Senegalese poet and politician Léopold Sédar Senghor, he rejects with one hand the French language and culture while taking these same things with the other. Like Senghor, Beauvoir could not reject the French cultural heritage because she is part of it or born into it. This would create a contradiction into her identity. Likewise, Beauvoir assumed an anti-French position as a French citizen in the face of atrocities committed by the French government and its citizens. This move—to assume an anti-French stance as a French citizen, reveals, like the Black poetry Sartre describes, the contradiction and tension in Beauvoir's position as a French colonial subject. As she said herself, others labeled her "anti-French," and she was subjected to numerous murder attempts for her personal and public position against French colonial rule. Beauvoir's *ressentiment* against French colonialism and torment about her Frenchness in the face of France's war crimes was not something she could hide from others—from other White French citizens.

In this book, I reveal the impact of French colonialism on Beauvoir, positing that it was during the Algerian War (1954–1962)—the last stages of French colonial rule—that Beauvoir grew into her role as a political activist. I document the development of her political consciousness, tracing Beauvoir's intellectual journey from being apolitical in the 1920s, as she was studying for her *aggregation*, to becoming political as part of the Resistance during World War II, to being a political intellectual and activist starting in the middle to late 1950s. Acknowledging her commitment to feminist activism after World War II—such as her participating in movements against the decrees of the Right Wing French government or in movements for abortion rights, will require being aware of how colonialism affected her political journey as a public intellectual. Indeed, Beauvoir was every bit as politically aware as her male peers Sartre and Fanon. She indicates the force of her political consciousness through her intellectual commitment to existential ethics and issues of gender and colonialism in the context of twentieth-century French philosophy.

Not only did Beauvoir's writings show us how she was able to make the political *personal*, but they also show how she was able to make the personal *political*. In her essays and memoirs, then, we gain a sense that the act of *telling everything,* or the act of narrating most aspects of her life, creates a sense of transparency between the author and the audience, which brings the acts of self-critique and critical analysis to a deeper level of understanding. How she confronted the status of her own gender in *The Second Sex*, the ways she debated her position on the trial and potential execution of Robert Brasillach in "An Eye for an Eye," how she revealed her White guilt complex as it affected her position on the lot of the colonized Algerians in *Force of Circumstance* are all examples of how Beauvoir made the personal *political* and political *personal*. From this perspective, we can claim that whatever thoughts Beauvoir had about her personal life was a matter of political inquiry. Extending the project of political writing, then, from discourse to first-person narratives, Beauvoir was able to influence the field of philosophy and the work of philosophers by contributing to how philosophers should become publicly and personally critical of their own subject position not only as potential oppressors but also as free political subjects who have the capacities to make the right choices—be they political and/or ethical—despite the contradictions and errors in their personal and public positions.

My project presents an alternative reading of Beauvoir as a feminist *colonial* intellectual rather than solely as a feminist intellectual. More specifically, born in France in 1908, and having an intellectual career that began to flourish in the 1940s, Beauvoir was always a subject of French colonialism; a political system that began in the fifteenth century with appropriation of land in the Western hemisphere and ended in 1977, with the independence France's last colony in Africa, Djibuti. The standard reading of Beauvoir, which can be found in the works of Margaret Simons, Emily Grosholz, Sonia Kruks, and Kristana Arp, for example, assumes that Beauvoir's feminist philosophy, especially during the last stage of French colonialism, is not necessarily influenced by this fierce political context. I argue instead that Beauvoir was not only concerned about French colonialism in itself, but that she also used French colonialism to elucidate women's oppression—or White women's oppression, more specifically, in the shadows of France's brutal colonial legacy. To assume that Beauvoir's work was not influenced by colonialism is an ethical and political error on the part of contemporary scholars. As such, I seek to directly intervene in these critical assumptions, reshaping and correcting Beauvoir's image as a political figure living during French imperial rule.

In the 1940s, Beauvoir was already intellectually concerned with colonialism. In *The Second Sex* and *The Ethics of Ambiguity,* Beauvoir mentions aspects of French and British colonialism. However, her take on the subject is still relatively passive. She was not vocal on the subject nor did she hold any press conferences about the problems with French colonialism. Only at the start of the Algerian War of Independence, in 1954, did Beauvoir begin to have an active role in the anti-colonial movements in France's territory. Her journey toward colonial consciousness is chronicled in her autobiography *Force of Circumstance.* Her failure to actively participate in the anti-colonial movements in France and her lack of interest in speaking up about the evils of colonialism point not to her neglectfulness of important social and political issues, but rather to the unintentional biases and privileges that enabled Beauvoir to remain publicly silent about the evils of colonialism and the rights and demands of the colonized after WWII, beginning with the start of the Indochina War in 1946 and ending her public silence at the start of the Algerian

War of Independence, in 1954. In this sense, we can see how Beauvoir started to formulate her views on colonialism from a position that reflected her *bad faith*; a position that alluded more to her pre-reflective consciousness than to her unconscious; a state of awareness that reveals that Beauvoir could not act against colonialism without giving serious thought to the question on French colonialism. I present Beauvoir's state of consciousness in this manner to give Beauvoir more responsibility for her unintentional biases or even unintentional racism. By framing my analysis in this introduction with terms such as a *bad faith, pre-reflective consciousness, intentional anti-racism,* and *unintentional biases/racism,* I present my criticism of Beauvoir on the colonial question in the Existentialist tradition, one that stems from the philosophical work of Sartre and a philosophical system that Beauvoir was very much a part of. As I argue, within the context of Existentialism, Beauvoir's position would indicate culpability and an act of bad faith. Furthermore, from this existential perspective, we can imagine that Beauvoir's unintentional racism and intentional anti-racist position within the system of French colonialism do not contradict but rather complement one another. The Existentialist tradition allows us to hold agents responsible for the intended *and* the unintended consequences of his or her actions. Through my analysis, we can begin to imagine how, during French colonialism, Beauvoir embodied both racist and anti-racist practices, despite the fact that she did not intend any act of racism when she chose at first to remain less vocal about the problems with French colonialism. But since Beauvoir chose finally to speak out, her commitment to anti-racism about the crimes of French colonialism warrants attention. Tracing the actions of Beauvoir on colonialism points to a phenomenological account of the events from which a White scholar can transition from racially problematic positions to fully embracing anti-racism. However, the transition is not as easy as it may seem, and Beauvoir's personal narratives illuminate just such a political and ethical transition.

It was not the cause of Vietnamese men and women but rather the cause of the Algerian men and women that incited Beauvoir to speak up. The events of 1954—the start of the Algerian War of Independence and the end of the Indochinese War—that drew Beauvoir[2] out of her position of privilege, in which she could have lived in France as a White woman, regardless for the discrimination and injustice against Asians, Arabs and Blacks, and still feel guilt-free about herself. Slowly, "she began seeing her role in politics differently as she wrote less than ten years later [in *Force of Circumstance*], she came to realize that, this time [in 1954], she 'wanted to be in the right side of history.'"[3] Reviewing Beauvoir's intellectual trajectory from the end of WWII until 1954 reveals how her lack of public engagement with the anti-colonial cause in France signals unintentional biases, or even unintentional racism;[4] indeed, her silence as an intellectual and a writer led to unintended

but still harmful consequences for the colonized, For example, to remain
silent as a public intellectual in the face of the atrocities the colonized faced in
the hands of French officials and in the hands of the average French citizens
in the colonies could be considered a form of indirect racism on the part of the
public intellectual, since the public intellectual's silence reveals her/his sense
of complicity with the system of colonialism. However, when Beauvoir got
out of her silence and began to speak against French colonialism, the French
public began to see how complex her complicity with the French regime was.
In other words, if Beauvoir had taken an unswerving public position on colonialism or written on the topic in less neutral terms—as she did in *The Ethics
of Ambiguity* and *The Second Sex*—she would have been outright against the
colonial system like some of her peers, most significantly, Sartre. According
to Sandrine Sanos, "In the wake of World War II, colonialism was now the
greatest injustice to fight against. Beauvoir thought a victory by Vietnamese nationalists against the French empire was a good thing and 'made her
happy.' But, unlike Jean-Paul Sartre, she did not write about this conflict."[5]
She just had lots of personal feelings against the system of colonialism.

In the early 1950s, when Paris became the cultural center of the politically
and ideologically charged Négritude Movement, Beauvoir did not contribute
to publications on the movement led by black Francophone writers—as Sartre
did with "Black Orpheus" and his work with the publication *Présence Afric-
aine*, created in Paris in 1947.[6] Beauvoir had many opportunities to speak up
about Algerian oppression—such as in 1945, when the French forces went
to Algeria and killed thousands of Algerians in retaliation for the Algerians'
protest against colonialism—an event that led to the death of about four
hundred French people. Beauvoir's privileged position as a White woman
essentially made her a colonizer, unintentionally culpable for the oppression of the colonized. After 1954, Beauvoir's position changed: her colonial
consciousness, which showed stirrings in in 1946 bloomed and spanned well
into the 1960s. This is the trajectory I chronicle in this book. In doing so, I
want to show the good and the bad of Beauvoir's colonial consciousness and
White privilege.

To present an unflinching narrative of how colonialism was implicated
and explicated in Beauvoir's writing, this project addresses four topics. The
first topic assesses Beauvoir's blindness to the *intersectionality* of race and
gender, as made apparent in her liaison with Djamila Boupacha, a member of
the Algerian National Liberation Front, and in her analysis of the Black slave
in *The Second Sex*. This ignorance, I argue, affected how Beauvoir considered
the situations and struggles of colonized women. Next, I look at her concerns
with or interest in the use and value of *violence* in post–World War France,
by the French against the colonized Other. Thirdly, I evaluate *The Second*

Sex's testimony of White women as "The Other" whose lived history is seen in terms of experiences of class, slavery, and racial oppression. Finally, I look at her commitment to an *inter-subjective ethics*. Because an examination of Beauvoir's intellectual journey during the French colonial era will point to the role of women in the political system, my main argument in this book is that some assessments of women's participation in the development of twentieth-century French colonial and intellectual thought must feature Simone de Beauvoir—either as a source of praise or a source of blame, or even shame.

Through these four topics, I address the themes of *freedom, identity*—in terms of gender, racial oppression, and white privilege—and *violence*. Covering these themes will show how, through Beauvoir's philosophical reflections, some women have thought about their identities in terms of the influence of colonial systems on their gender and racial oppression and/or privilege. I attempt to show how Beauvoir can serve as an interlocutor to the themes of *freedom, violence,* and *identity* that framed the conditions for women during the last stages of French colonialism. My primary interest in Beauvoir's philosophy is how she explicated issues of colonialism in terms of women's lived experiences, not just the lives of White French women but also the situation of women of color, such as the Arab woman Djamila Boupacha. Though I certainly find faults with the way Beauvoir relates colonialism to gender oppression, my analysis shows—as Beauvoir's philosophical expositions did—that there cannot be a discussion of French colonialism without accounting for the roles of women, White or non-White, within that system. The gender dynamics in the later stages of the French colonial empire cannot be separated from studies of the intellectual history of French colonialism.

Situating Beauvoir at the center stage of the colonial analysis in this book shows how women have participated in the developments of colonialism and how women have fought against the evils of colonialism. In view of these concerns, my project addresses the following questions: *What insight can we gain if we closely examine what the intellectual history of French colonialism would look like if we focused on women? How would women decipher the crimes of colonialism? How are the colonial themes concerning freedom, violence, and identity deciphered in the thoughts of women?* To this end, I conclude that *some* discussions on French colonialism ought to be centered on the relations between colonized women and colonizer women to present alternative narratives on colonization. By undertaking such a tack, I hope to push feminist philosophy and post-colonial philosophy toward inter-subjective and intersectional analyses, which are more closely aligned to the female experience. Also, I use the female experience as an approach that can serve a better understanding of the intellectual history of French colonialism toward the end of French colonial rule.

OUTLINE OF CHAPTERS

I here provide an outline of the project in order to present the scope of this study. Following my analysis of the themes of *freedom, violence,* and *identity,* I will separate the main body of my thesis into two parts. The first part, "First Philosophy," comprises chapters 2 and 3 and speaks to Beauvoir's reflections on freedom vis-à-vis women's gender identity. The second part, "Discourse of Colonialism," includes chapters 4 and 5, and unpacks Beauvoir's explications of violence as it relates to women's identity, based on both racial oppression and White privilege. I argue that what Beauvoir adds to the study of French colonialism is the possibility of understanding and sharing reflections of women on the subjects of colonialism, particularly on freedom, identity, and violence. A closer look at these specific reflections will reveal the limitations of exclusively drawing upon the narratives and reflections of men on the dominant dialectic between White men and colonized men.

Chapter 1, "The Dominant 'French Intellectual' Post-Colonial Philosophy," situates my project within the dominant discourses of post-colonial philosophy and feminist philosophy. I present a review of the literature on post-colonial philosophy and feminist philosophy and explain why there are more studies on Sartre and Fanon on the French colonial question than on Beauvoir. I present a brief overview of the scholarship on gender, race, sex, and colonialism by (1) explaining why Sartre is not interested in feminism and how this very lack of interest affected his representation of both White women and non-White women in his philosophical texts; and by (2) elucidating why Fanon's representation of White women and non-White women does not necessarily do justice to the social situations of these women. The goal of this exposition is to show what is lacking in the works of Fanon and Sartre—such as discussions of the relationships among women during colonial times—and how a post-colonial study of Beauvoir's work can attempt to fill this gap. In chapter 2, "*The Second Sex*: Beauvoir's First Famous Colonial Text," I offer a reading of this pivotal feminist work as a colonial text that situates White women in France as *colons*. Here, I show how some aspects of the position of colonizer women relates to the situation of colonized women. This chapter and the one that follows are interconnected. In chapter 2, I focus on the liberal political rights—specifically the voting rights—of White women in France; I then focus on the liberal political rights, or the freedom, of non-White women in France's territories.

In chapter 3, "The Others' Other: Towards an Inter-Subjective Ethics," I examine the inter-subjective nature of the concept of freedom in Beauvoir and Sartre and conceptualize how this type of analysis could give voice to the freedom of colonized women in France's territories. Specifically, I look at the interconnection among Sartre's, Beauvoir's, and Paulette Nardal's positions on the concept of freedom. This perspective will more clearly map out how

Beauvoir's inter-subjective ethics can, in part, work as a substitute for the lack of intersectional analysis in her philosophy. After this chapter, the reader will have a better understanding of how colonialism has the potential to politically oppress both White women and non-White women, making these women less politically free, despite their intention to actively fight the injustices of colonialism. In chapter 4, "Colonial Trends: On Violence," I present a comparative analysis between Beauvoir's conception of violence and Fanon's. I set my analysis in this manner because Fanon's analysis on violence dominates the field of post-colonial philosophy, especially when it comes to the status of French colonialism within the field of philosophy. If Beauvoir is compared to Fanon perhaps contemporary scholars of feminism and post-colonial philosophy might begin to pay attention to Beauvoir's view of violence in the same manner that other female authors, such as Hannah Arendt, have been given credit for productively exploring the subject of violence in the twentieth century.

In chapter 5, "Beauvoir's Problem: White Guilt/Privilege and, Gender and Race Intersectionality," I present an analysis of Beauvoir's involvement in the Boupacha trial and how her perspective on this even affected Beauvoir's subject position as a White woman living under French colonialism. I draw a comparative analysis between Beauvoir's and Halimi's position on the case of Djamila Boupacha in order to show the difference of opinions between these two women despite their collaborative efforts to free Boupacha. In the concluding chapter, chapter 6, "Toward an Inclusive Beauvoirian Scholarship," I examine Beauvoir's work on colonialism in terms of current political interventions by White women on the part of non-White women. I also present a critique of certain aspects of contemporary scholarship on Beauvoir, which in turn represents a more general, entrenched failure among White female authors to consider the circumstances of non-White women because they either omit important the suggestive intersectionalities within the situation of non-White women or fail to consider the case of non-White women in any in-depth way. In the end, I study Stephanie Rivera Berruz's article on the relation of Latina identity to Beauvoir's *The Second Sex*, in order to show the promise of contemporary scholarship on Beauvoir.

Before I move on to the body of this book, I want to assert that the literature review that follows not only attempts to cover the scholarship on Beauvoir and French colonialism and its intersection with race and gender in particular, but also attempts to look specifically at such research within the field of philosophy; it does not focus on the prominent and more reviewed topic of Beauvoir on slavery and its intersection to race and gender. While of course not all aspects of Beauvoir's analysis of French colonialism can be separated from her argument on slavery (as it is presented in *The Second Sex*), I make the effort to tease out Beauvoir's analysis on colonialism and its imbrications with race and gender from the prominent and more reviewed topic of Beauvoir on slavery and its intersection with race and gender, simply because, and at least in the United States, Beauvoir's analysis on colonialism is less explored than her analysis on slavery.

What I claim here shows the intentions of my analysis and signals that I believe more scholarship in the United States needs to be done on the work of Beauvoir in relation to French colonialism. Also, my choice to focus on colonialism instead of slavery in Beauvoir's work is based on my belief that race and gender relations under slavery are not the same as race and gender relations under colonialism. Indeed, I am wary of the slavery-colonialism analogy that assumes that whatever race and gender relations that occurred under slavery also occurred under colonialism, e.g., that most slaves were forced to work for free while the majority of the colonized were forced to work for meager wages or how most slaves lost their ability to speak tribal languages with their community members as they did back in the African continent while, there were some exceptions, the colonized knew both their tribal language and the language of Europeans. My goal in this book is to study aspects of the situation of colonized and colonizer women primarily within the context of French colonialism.

NOTES

1. Although I consider my project to be an intervention into the extant scholarship on Beauvoir and French colonialism, it also seeks to complement the comparative analyses featured in Jonathan Judaken's edited collection, *Race after Sartre* (2008), Paige Arthur's *Unfinished Projects: Decolonization and the Philosophy of Jean-Paul Sartre* (London: Verso, 2010), and Kathryn T. Gines, "Sartre, Beauvoir, and the Race/ Gender Analogy,"—(presently known as Kathryn Sophia Belle) article on Sartre and Beauvoir as featured in *Convergences: Black Feminism and Continental Philosophy*, ed. Maria del Guadalupe Davidson, Kathryn T. Gines, and Donna-Dale L. Marcano (New York, NY: SUNY Press 2010). Also, this book intends to be comparable to the work of Margaret Simons, *Beauvoir and The Second Sex: Feminism, Race, and the Origins of Existentialism* (Lanham, MD: Rowman & Littlefield Publishers, 1999), Sandrine Sanos's *Simone de Beauvoir: Creating a Feminist Existence in the World* (New York, NY: Oxford University Press, 2016), and the authors featured in the anthology *Simone de Beauvoir's Political Thinking* (2006), edited by Lori Jo Marso and Patricia Moynagh. Given my research interests in these authors, I pick Paige Arthur's research in order to compare and give an example of the analysis that my research adds to post-colonial philosophy, feminism and the scholarship on Beauvoir.

2. Sanos, *Simone de Beauvoir*, 112.

3. Ibid.

4. Naomi Zack, *Thinking about Race* (Belmont, CA: Thomson Wadsworth, 2006), 49.

5. Sanos, *Simone de Beauvoir*, 109.

6. Ibid., 110.

Part I

THE SITUATION, POST-COLONIAL PHILOSOPHY, AND BEAUVOIR

Chapter 1

The Dominant "French Intellectual" Postcolonial Philosophy

When we consider thinkers and philosophers who have influenced the intellectual history of French colonialism in the twentieth century, Jean-Paul Sartre and Frantz Fanon dominate the field. For the most part, Simone de Beauvoir's contributions to thinking on issues of gender and colonialism as they relate to freedom, violence, and identity receive very little consideration. While scholars such as Margaret Simons have described Beauvoir's view on gender, race, and existentialism,[1] very little extended study attends to Beauvoir's analysis of gender, race, and colonialism, in itself, and then in comparison to the work of Sartre and Fanon, respectively. As exceptions, we find studies such as that of continental philosopher Kathryn Gines, whose essay "Sartre, Beauvoir and the Race/Gender Analogy," compares the analysis of racial oppression by Sartre to Beauvoir's. However, while Gines's analysis contributes to continental philosophy and critical race philosophy, it examines Beauvoir and Sartre's outlook on racial and gender oppression primarily within the racialized context of the United States, and not in terms of French colonialism.[2] Gines's most recent article on Beauvoir, published in 2014, follows the same discursive trends—tending to the question of gender oppression as it relates to the intersectional conditions of the slave and/or Black woman, specifically in *The Second Sex*,[3] in order to discuss how the text relates to analyses of slavery. Gines's article begins with a comparative framework between gender oppression and colonialism as well as racism, antisemitism, and/or class oppression. However, her analysis shines the most when she examines the various ways Beauvoir describes White women as slaves or enslaved despite the skin privilege of being White.[4] Gines's study of the colonized subject within Beauvoirian philosophy is more tied to a critique of the anti-Semite and the proletariat and the interconnection among the three. In sum, her scholarship speaks more to issues relating to White women in the narrative of "woman as slave" than to the analogy of gender oppression to the situation colonized subjects. Furthermore, in *A Companion to Simone de Beauvoir*, published in 2017, despite the fact the authors of the anthology attempt to present innovative trends on the study of Beauvoir's philosophy, there is no section or let alone a paper solely dedicated to the views of Beauvoir on French colonialism. Although in the anthology, Kathryn Gines, Lori J. Marso, and Shannon Sullivan's articles speak on the importance of studying Beauvoir's philosophy in terms of colonial themes, such as race, gender, and violence, there are no extensive analyses in their articles on how French colonialism as a system influenced the philosophy of Beauvoir.[5]

Beauvoir's view on gender, race, and colonialism have also been studied through her involvement in the case of Djamila Boupacha, a young Algerian women and member of the National Liberation Front, who was sentenced to death by the French government after being accused of planting a bomb in the European quarters in Algeria. In "Beauvoir and the Case of Djamila Boupacha," Mary Caputi presents the work of Sartre and Fanon in relation to Beauvoir's fight against the imprisonment of Boupacha as a way of discussing Beauvoir's political involvement during the Algerian War as a reflection of Beauvoir's altruism.[6] However, in presenting Beauvoir this way, Caputi shows Beauvoir's anti-colonial position as isolated within her own intellectual trajectory, a position from which the anti-colonial movement in France cannot be examined and discourses on the relation among gender, race, and colonialism cannot be further examined. We do not speak of Sartre's and Fanon's stand against French colonialism as altruistic; indeed, their condemnation of French colonialism is seen as political or even revolutionary. It is this approach to Sartre's and Fanon's stance against French colonialism that I want to emphasize in my analysis of Beauvoir, which is lacking in Caputi's article. Caputi presents Beauvoir in favorable light. However, it should be noted that, according to Caputi's analysis, Beauvoir's anti-colonial position says more about her subject position as a French woman colonizer than about her critical take on the colonized. Yet, a closer examination of Beauvoir's anti-colonialism signals a balanced position between her own place as a White woman colonizer and that of many colonized Arab women. First, Beauvoir's criticism of colonialism reflects her ethics and politics. Indeed, Beauvoir argued that one could not experience the social and political circumstances of his or her time without being publicly concerned about them and getting involved. This means that one must take some sort of *stand* about the issues of their time, even if it's a dismissive or antagonistic one. We must engage in some way, even if the engagement is disengagement. After the Second World War, Beauvoir wrote an article titled "An Eye for an Eye" in order to address what ought to be done with French collaborators. In another case, during the Algerian War, Beauvoir wrote in *Force of*

Circumstance about the ways the position of the French intellectual was compromised because of France's involvement with the killing and torture of the Algerians. At this time, Beauvoir argued that it was impossible to support the cause of the French in Algeria without feeling like a collaborator. Based on these examples, Beauvoir's ethics and politics indicate that the position of the French intellectual was, at times, contradictory—the French intellectual ought to remain French while being critical of the flaws of French society. Therefore, the French intellectual must continuously confront the inherent dilemma and contradiction within French society.

Secondly, Beauvoir's involvement in the Boupacha trial shows her attempt to depict the sense of agency and responsibility that colonized women possess—even from within their own oppressed situations. In *Force of Circumstance,* for example, Beauvoir's attempt to relate the context of colonialism to her own situation, and then to the situation of Gisele Halimi and Djamila Boupacha, shows concrete concern for the ways colonialism contributes to gender oppression.[7] Beauvoir's writing on colonialism provides a unique insight into the position and interaction of women within the French colonial system; unfortunately, this elucidation is rarely given the attention it deserves. While I praise Caputi for discussing Beauvoir's engagement with issues of French colonialism, more can be done—specifically, trying to understand Beauvoir and her philosophy about women who are subjects of colonialism.

In view of the (however scant) recent publications that take as their focus Beauvoir's analysis of race, gender, and colonialism, I want to focus precisely on those parts of Beauvoir's writings that allude to these topics. I form my analysis on race, gender, and colonialism within similar theoretical framework as those presented on the works of Fanon and Sartre; that is, through the lens of postcolonial philosophy and the relation of colonialism to politics, ethics, economics, gender, race, culture, and psychoanalysis. As a distinct scholarly effort, my project situates Beauvoir's work in this same constellation of issues. The difference between Fanon's and Sartre's analyses and Beauvoir's reflections on French colonialism is, as I show, that to Beauvoir, French colonialism is based more on sets of interpersonal relations and less as a political and economic system. As such, one may talk about how her deliberations on French colonialism intersect with the personal and political situations of women.

Following the approach that French colonialism is more about sets of interpersonal relationships than about a political and economic system, I argue that the gender dynamics—an example of interpersonal relationships but not devoid of political and class conflicts among women—cannot be separated from studies of French colonialism. I look at Beauvoir's work as well as at the secondary literature on Beauvoir to discuss the intellectual history of French colonialism and how it presents the position and situation of women—as

either colonized or colonizer. Predominantly, the intellectual history of twentieth-century French colonialism that focuses on Sartre and Fanon, especially
during the last stages of French colonialism, primarily looks at the dialectic
between European and non-European men, presenting analyses of French
colonialism that are too systematic and lacking interpersonal considerations.
Analyses of French colonialism undertaken with a systematic approach will
lead to studies based more on the dominant members of a society—the male
subject position for the most part. Looking at French colonialism through an
interpersonal approach can yield a more nuanced study by not only focusing
on the dominant members of a society, but also its subservient and disadvantaged members. While Sartre and Fanon are essential to philosophical arguments against the institution of colonialism, their analyses ignore fully half
the populations of both colonizing Europeans and the colonized non-Europeans. Explicating the human impact of the French colonial empire solely
through the lens of Sartre and Fanon perpetuates discourses that assume that
the colonial system is primarily determined by the condition of colonized
men and male colonizers.

Sartre's position on colonialism is primarily formed by his subject position
as a White male colonizer, as he described himself for as long as the French
system of colonialism was in place. As a crucial element of his anti-colonial
stand, Sartre denied the view common among the French that, though the
system of colonialism was in place within France's political institution, the
French could always claim that some colonizers were *good*, though there
were wicked ones among them. Writing while colonialism was fully operat-
ing, Sartre stated a position on colonialism that I support: the French were just
colons, there's no meaningful distinction between good or bad ones.[8]

Fanon's position on colonialism is formed by his subject position as a colonized Black man who is inhumanely reduced to that identity. In *Black Skin,
White Masks*, published in 1952, he describes how, because of his race and
color, he is objectified by a White French boy in a train.[9] Fanon keenly felt
his position in the world as a racialized and colonial subject.

Nonetheless, in view of their position as male subjects, both Fanon and
Sartre enjoyed the privilege of overlooking how the gender and power
dynamics in the French empire were affected by patriarchy—the patriarchy
of White men *and* the patriarchy of men of color. A considerable failure in
Sartre's arguments on the colonial condition is the universal and gender-
neutral standpoint from which he attempts to depict and analyze the condition of the colonized and the colonizers as groups of people. During this
period, he wrote a series of articles; one piece, titled *The Critique,* is on the
subject of the Algerian liberation, 1950s to 1961, a time in which Algerian
women did not have the right to vote.[10] In his arguments for the political
enfranchisement of the colonized, Sartre does not question the lack of
political rights among Algerian women. Sartre's questions on the political

subjectivity of the colonized did not include the political subjectivity of colonized women, who were excluded from the liberal political system through a triple disadvantage: the average level of their education, their race, and their gender.

In his essay "Colonialism is a System," Sartre observes that the desire for French nationals to maintain control over the colony meant that the right to vote granted to Muslim men had been tampered with because Muslim men outnumbered French men in post–Second World War Algeria.[11] Sartre's analysis assumes that if Muslim men in Algeria could not secure the right to vote and forge a political voice under the system of colonialism, then neither could Muslim women. However, this analysis does not consider the liberal political reality that, among a group of people, the male members have acquired political rights before the female members.[12] Historically, this political phenomenon can be observed in the United States, in France and Martinique, for examples. Just as Algerian Muslim men were forced to fight for what was unquestioningly granted to French men, both Algerian and French women were excluded from membership in the decision-making class.

Precisely because Sartre does not explicitly discuss the problems of the liberal political inequality of Algerian women, we cannot assume that what he says of the Muslim population applies to Muslim women. Sartre's argument on the colonial condition of colonized men does not necessarily imply that he is arguing for improvements to the condition of colonized women. On those few occasions that Sartre might seem to consider the position of women, he tends to conflate the condition of women with that of men, and that of all men with his own particular condition. When, in 1975, Beauvoir questioned Sartre about why, despite his concern for the condition of the oppressed, he never talked about women as an oppressed group, Sartre responded:

> I think it dates back to my childhood, when I was more or less surrounded by women. My grandmother and my mother took care of me, and I was also surrounded by little girls. So that girls and women in some way formed my naturalized environment, and I have always believed that there was some sort of woman inside me.[13]

In this somewhat eccentric explanation, Sartre explains himself by saying that, having been cared for by women, femaleness became "naturalized" to the point that he does not characteristically draw gender distinctions. Indeed, any differences between male and female are blurred to the point that he himself embodies femaleness. However, another result of this somewhat audacious explanation is that Sartre became indifferent to the differences between the sexes. I'd add that he seems to think this was a good thing.

Sartre's answer to Beauvoir asserts that issues of domination and subordination within the relation between male and female did not influence his analysis on oppression—indeed he does not seem to notice them at all. Overlooking any differences between French male and female subjects, I claim, enabled Sartre to ignore the discrepancies between male and female colonized subjects as well. As Beauvoir asserts in the interview, Sartre had a blind spot where the conditions of women were concerned.[14]

Unlike Sartre, Fanon explicitly wrote about the colonial condition of women. We cannot forget the two well-known chapters in *Black Skin, White Masks* that discuss, first, the relations between women of color and White men and, second, the relations between men of color and White women.[15] However, as has been shown, for example, in T. Denean Sharpley-Whiting's studies of Fanon, the language that Fanon uses to articulate interracial relation exposes his own racial and sexual biases more than it confers a realistic depiction of race and sexual relations among the male and female subjects of the colonized-colonizer population.[16]

Among the problems with Fanon's analysis is that his language reveals the disjunction that he experienced between the relations of colonized men to colonized women. As expressed in *Black Skin White Masks*, Fanon never compares the alienation of Black men to the alienation of Black women. Precisely because of these gaps in Fanon's analysis, the gender politics from which he examines the condition of colonized women in *Black Skin White Masks* are completely debilitating. He fails to facilitate a critical examination of colonialism that takes into consideration women in the French colonial empire. Indeed, Fanon's position on Algerian women—that is, describing Algerian women with a sense of agency and a sense of purpose within colonial Algeria—has come under scrutiny by feminist postcolonial scholars. Marie-Aime Helie-Lucas, Anne McClintock, Diane Fuss, and T. Denean Sharpley-Whiting have variously posited that Fanon problematically exaggerates the possible freedom and liberation of Algerian women. Despite praising Fanon for mentioning the circumstances of Algerian women, these scholars criticize Fanon for presenting a false sense of empowerment among Algerian women. Indeed, Fanon's writing on the participation of Arab women in the Algerian War was definitely reflected a feminist intervention on records concerning the agency and political freedom of Arab women during colonial times. However, participation in the sphere of war did not guarantee Arab women freedom in the private and public spheres, and this is why contemporary feminists have criticized Fanon.

To Fanon, assuming that the colonizers are already politically liberated, that is they live in a world of their own choosing, the subject of freedom is the non-European man and in exceptional and extraordinary cases, such as the case of Arab women in Algeria, some non-European women. Fanon's analysis in *Black Skin, White Masks*, *The Wretched of the Earth* and in *A Dying Colonialism* suggests that freedom and political liberation among the colonized is possible only when the colonized have taken charge of the corruptive elements within their situations. To Fanon, the corruptive elements within the situation of the colonized reflect the insurgences of Western ideal and norm, such as education, medicine, language, and racism that dehabilitate the growth of the colonized.[17] From Fanon's analysis, we learn that among non-Europeans, male colonized "elite" and women of color in general are the most corrupted in the sense that they are more apt to allow Western ideal and norms to corrupt their political choices and lifestyle. Fanon's analysis of black nationalist leaders in *The Wretched of the Earth* and his analysis of women of color through Mayotte Capécia in *Black Skin, White Masks*, shows his concern with the ways in which assimilation de-habilitates the freedom of the colonized. Furthermore, in view of my analysis on the politics and ethics of Paulette Nardal, the fact that she was Christian and endorsed humanist and political liberal principles would have made her suspect within Fanon's conception of political liberation. We cannot forget that like Nardal, Fanon participated in the political campaigns of Martinique, particularly in Aimé Césaire's 1946 campaign, under the auspices of the French Communist Party, for the position as the prime minister of Martinique.[18] Yet, already in his participation in the campaign of Césaire, Fanon was already critical and anticipated that the election of Césaire would not be the solution to the systematic racial discrimination experienced by the mass population of blacks within the French political system.[19] Unlike Nardal then, even in his participation in the campaign of Césaire, Fanon kept himself at a distance to the values of political liberalism precisely because he saw that the election of Césaire would not make black citizens a normative subject of political liberalism. Among colonized women and even among the colonized as a whole, Fanon uninhibitedly analyzed the condition Arab women in Algeria as being capable of freedom precisely because he viewed the situation of women in Algeria as being on average less corrupted by Western ideals and norms, and more influenced by the patriarchal order established by Arab men. To Fanon then, the problem of freedom and political liberation is the problem of assimilation. However, given the way Fanon's freedom and political liberation is based on the racial and gender oppression of the colonized, his analysis attests to the problem with describing racial and gender oppression from a perspective that focuses on the problem of racial integration while leaving aside the various ways in which the oppressed themselves have sought to be assimilated as a way of acquiring political liberation. Thus from Fanon's analysis, we gather that Western ideals and norms are rarely ever beneficial within the situation of the colonized. He would say, as he examined his own situation as a psychiatrist,[20] the mastery of Western ideals and norms within the situation of the colonized creates social and racial complexes for the colonized, and these disgraces within the lives of the colonized, outweigh the benefits of assimilation. Fanon's explanation then, would conflict with the ways that female colonized writers such as Mayotte Capécia, Paulette Nardal, and Assia Djebar, although they have supported the anticolonialist movement dominated by male-colonized leaders, have dealt with social and racial complexes, and have dealt with social discrimination, have also chosen to be educated in Western institutions and mastered the French language in order to acquire freedom (a chosen life, a job, and a purpose) for themselves; a freedom that resulted in their active political and literary attempt to forge the possibility of political liberation within the gender and racial oppression of colonized women and to forge a space from which women can face lived reality.

The chapter, which was specifically centered on the writings of the female Martinican writer, Mayotte Capécia, claimed to examine parts of the colonial reality of women of color from the perspective of the author's fictive writing, which Fanon assumed to an autobiography of the author herself despite the evidence.[21] Instead of examining the racial internalization of women of color from the socio-olitical complex of the French political system, Fanon examined the racial internalization of women of color from the perspective of the sexual-psychological state of their relationship with men, and more particularly with white men, whereby those among women of color who choose have sexual relationship with white men, did so as a way of conferring their desire to leave black men behind[22] and their desire to be white[23] or just the desire to have a little of bit of whiteness in their lives.[24]

As T. Denean Sharpley-Whiting notes, Fanon's use of language to articulate the racial-sexualized situations of women of color has come under scrutiny,[25] by scholars such as Christiane P. Makward,[26] Rey Chow[27] and also by Sharpley-Whiting herself. Nonetheless, Sharpley-Whiting asserts that Fanon was neither silent on the question of gender nor sexually indifferent.[28] Yet, it is precisely Fanon's non-indifference to the sexuality and gender of women color that barred him from carefully examining the manner in which the sexual differences between black men and women affects the colonial condition of women of color.

As Rey Chow notes, an issue with Fanon's analysis on the women of color is that he assumed that what applies to one woman of color can also apply to any other, such that the differences between the author, Capécia, and her female characters have no significance within his analysis.[29] Making the same error that Sartre made in examining the faces of Chinese women, whom he saw as expressing the identical feeling as the faces of women in Marseilles, Algeria, or London, Fanon assumed that the fictional life of a woman of color could resemble the real life of any other woman of color.

Furthermore, given the literary stature of Capécia at the time, the fact that in 1949 she would become the fourth Antillean and the first black women to be awarded the renowned *Grand Prix Littéraire des Antilles* for *Je Suis*

Martiniquaise published in 1948,[30] it is quite odd that if Fanon was perplexed by her writing, he did not make the effort to communicate with Capécia regarding her motivations, nor did he attempt to do thorough research on the author. Moreover, since Fanon was familiar with the negritude movement and with the movement's concern for the cultural and literary expression of blacks, he could have attempted to collaborate with Suzanne Césaire in particular, another Martinican women author, in order to have a public dialogue about the value of having another black women such as Capécia who came to the forefront of Antillean literature by winning the *Grand Prix Littéraire*.

By choosing to examine the colonial condition of women of color from the writings of a black female author that he contested and disliked, Fanon addressed the question of gender differences among black men and women from the cultural biases that marginalized black women authors in Martinique.[31] What I say here should not suggest that I am against Fanon writing about a black female author that he dislikes. But, in comparison to his analysis of men of color that he presents through the writings of René Maran whose books Fanon preferred, his analysis of René Maran shows that unlike his interests for Capécia's writing, the purpose of including the works of René Maran in *Black Skin White Masks* was to examine the alienation of black men, a topic that was aligned to his main thesis on the non-integration and non-assimilation of black within the French political system,[32] and he also examined the work of René Maran in order to put into question the prejudices and taboos associated with the sexuality of black men.[33] On the other hand, Fanon's analysis of women of color through the works of Capécia did not integrate the condition of black women within the greater whole of his analysis on black alienation, nor did it challenge prejudices and taboos that codified the sexual aims of women of color. Ultimately, Fanon's analysis of Capécia further marginalized and mis-characterized black women writers in Martinique, and in his rebuttal of Capécia, Fanon's analysis were neither fair nor comprehensive. Therefore, even as a criticism of women of color, Fanon's analysis is not adequate, precisely because the motives of his analysis on Capécia are still very perplexing.

At the very most, from the analysis of Fanon we can only gather the claim that women of color are sexually liberated. However, the freedom that they acquire from being able to choose sexual partners who can potentially be other than a black man, only further binds these women to a state of disillusion and corruption; a disillusioned and corrupted state in which these women commit the act of seeking self-recognition beyond the boundaries of the black male figure. To Fanon, women of color who seek freedom and self-recognition beyond the boundaries of the black male figure are doomed to a state of *bad faith*; a state from which they can neither access or describe their condition as blacks. From this perspective then, even the fictional narratives of Capécia on women of color in Martinique only gives insight to the false sense of race-consciousness of women of color. From the false sense of race-consciousness of women of color then, the political prospects of people of color cannot be examined as a whole. Thus to Fanon, the writing of Capécia is only reflexive of the corruptive element within the intellectual development of writers who are also women of color, whereby these women could favor Western values, and the white man over the black man.

An exception to the marginalization of women writers in Martinique may have been the case of Suzanne Césaire, who not only collaborated with her husband at the time, Aimé Césaire, in the foundation and publications of *Tropiques*, a literary review founded to reflect the cultural and political ideas embodied by the negritude movement, and with other authors such as André Breton on the question of Martinique and Surrealism. Instead of just being given a few pages to present her works within black and creole literary publications, or just being allowed to publish books, Suzanna Césaire, unlike Capécia, was allowed to enter the circle of male writers and intellectuals from which she could communicate with them and have her voice be potentially heard among them. Yet within colonial and neocolonial studies, it has been shown by for example Sharpley-Whiting in *Negritude Women* that the contribution of Suzanne Césaire within the negritude movement has been less emphasized than the accomplishment of Aimé Césaire, and of other black male intellectuals such as Léopold Senghor.[34]

The condition of women of color is an understated problem within Fanon's thesis on the alienation of people of color in the Western political system, precisely because he believes that the real Other for the white man and his political system, as Anne McClintock notes, is and will continue to be the black man.[35] Fanon's body of work focuses on non-European men because he sees them as the most disruptive element within the Western political system. According to Fanon then, racial oppression is analogous to the oppression of black men only. What I mean to suggest here is that Fanon's examination on the women of color closed a potential collaborative dialogue among men and women and specifically between black men and black women. The closed dialogue between black men and black women featured in *Black Skin, White Masks* gave insight on the political status of women of color, and to the voice of women of color within the French political system. Politically, the analysis of Fanon on Capécia showed that the voice women of color in Martinique had yet to be heard.

Precisely because of the shortcomings of Sartre and Fanon on the relation of racial oppression to gender oppression, I consider the work of Beauvoir in order to bridge the gap within each of their analyses I am not claiming that including the work of Beauvoir on the questions of women and of colonialism will shed conclusive light on the condition of women in the colonial context, in general, or of colonized women, in particular. Instead, I assert that the discussions on sex, gender, and—at times—race initiated by Beauvoir and other philosophical postcolonial and feminist literature offers an alternative perspective that cannot manifest solely through Sartre's and Fanon's theories.

The gendered and racial dimensions of the case of a Tunisian woman lawyer Gisele Halimi, who approached Beauvoir in order to gain public recognition and political momentum to reverse the prison sentence of an Algerian woman FLN member, Djamila Boupacha, cannot be fully realized by only consulting the work of Fanon and Sartre. What does it mean for a colonized professional woman to demand the assistance of a European woman intellectual, or, indeed, of a woman colonizer? What does it mean for a woman colonizer to decide to come to the assistance of a colonized woman? What does it mean for a colonized professional woman to muster the resources she needs to help free a colonized Arab woman from prison? What does it mean for a woman professional to seek the assistance of a European woman precisely because she witnessed this woman come to the assistance of another European woman? Questions such as these, which can potentially provide insight into woman-to-woman interaction within the French colonial system—from various positions among and between colonizers and colonized—cannot be resolved through a colonial analysis solely centered on the works of Fanon and Sartre.

Even Fanon's analysis of the relation between non-Europeans and European women within the French empire is inadequate precisely because his sexist and demeaning views of European women perpetuates gender bias and gender oppression against European women. This dynamic is made clear by Traci C. West in her contribution to *Convergences: Black Feminism and Continental Philosophy*.[36] Through the works of Beauvoir, then, I claim that we may achieve a better representation of the condition of European women—as oppressed by virtue of their gender and as women subject to White privilege, White racism, and colonial power through birth. My analysis of the works of Beauvoir realizes a better assessment of the specific, contradictory, and coherent ways European women contributed to both the backing and the abolition of the French colonial system.

I should note that focusing on the works of Beauvoir gives rise to problems concerning "Imperial Feminism"; how the experience of White women in this subfield, as opposed to the lived histories of minority women that has led to the formation of the subfield of Black Feminism or Third World Feminism, dominates the field of Feminism. As both Valerie Amos and Pratibha Parmar argue in "Challenging Imperial Feminism," the failure by many White feminists to acknowledge the differences between themselves and Black and Third World women has contributed to the predominantly Eurocentric and ethnocentric theories of women's oppression.[37] The dominance of

White women's perspectives within feminist thought has refused differences between the oppressive conditions of Black and Third World women and the oppressive conditions of White women. To Amos and Parmar, then, "Imperial Feminism" is the imposition of the White female perspective on the study of all women's oppression. Along similar lines, I examine how Beauvoir's early conception of freedom exposes itself to the very criticism Amos and Parmar articulate. The concept of freedom that Beauvoir acquires through her analysis of the condition of French European women, which she presents specifically in *The Second Sex* and in *The Ethics of Ambiguity*, perpetuates an analysis of gender oppression that privileges the position of White women. In these texts, and in her reflections on the condition of White French women, in particular, Beauvoir argues that the situated condition of women limits their possible freedom or their ability to act as responsible agents.

However, there is a difference between the ways Beauvoir conceived of freedom and the ways French minority authors, such as Paulette Nardal, conceived of it. To Beauvoir, a person's freedom cannot be derived from his or her situation as an oppressed subject. Beauvoir has a traditional view that makes freedom and oppression mutually exclusive. However, she developed her concept of freedom to emphasize that if you are oppressed, you are not free only if you do not assess the situation of your oppression. For Nardal, it is precisely an individual's situation as an oppressed person that allows the person to claim his or her freedom. The contributions of Paulette Nardal to understanding the condition of colonized women, for example, support my criticism of Beauvoir's conception of freedom. Nardal chose to come to the assistance of non-European women who were oppressed despite the fact she was also subject to such oppression. The differences between Beauvoir's and Nardal's conceptions of freedom highlight Amos and Parmar's primary criticism of the establishment of White feminism. From this established position, Beauvoir's views on the limitation to freedom for women in France can eclipse any agency and responsibility that non-European women acquire, by virtue of their gender and racially subordinated position.

Sonia Kruks notes in her article "Simone de Beauvoir and the Politics of Privilege" that Beauvoir's critical approach to privilege, including her own, is based upon her analysis of the relations of human beings to their situations.[38] For Beauvoir, as Kruks states, "human beings are always selves 'in situation' our actions are once constrained *and* free; and second, she insists that situated human action is always *ambiguous* in its practical and moral import."[39] Even when human beings enjoy privilege, they are still bound by the ambiguous context and constraints of their situations. Kruks proceeds to address the issue of privilege in Beauvoir's writing in a later publication.[40] In this publication, *Simone de Beauvoir and the Politics of Ambiguity*, Kruks discusses how, according to Beauvoir, the privileged are able to think about their situation with honesty and without self-delusion. The autobiography of Beauvoir, *Force of Circumstance*, reflects just this.

In her autobiography, *Force of Circumstance*, Beauvoir admits that it was not of her own free will that she allowed the war in Algeria to invade her thoughts, her sleep, and her every mood.[41] In asserting that the Algerian War was not a subject she light-heartedly chose to write about, or intellectually concern herself with, Beauvoir admits to her privilege: she could have lived in France without ever *having* to write about the Algerian War. Yet, as she notes, given her role as an intellectual who took words and the truth to be of value, she could not in good faith have lived in France at the time without addressing the problems with the propaganda spread by French administrators about the people and the events of the Algerian War.[42] In view of the French administration's accounts of the Algerians and Algerian War, Beauvoir claims, "my own situation with regard to my country, to the world, to myself, was completely altered by it all."[43] Beauvoir's convictions in the midst of the Algerian War were affected by the pernicious difference between description of Algerians' actions propagated by French administrators and the true condition of the Algerians. From this perspective, we gain an understanding that Beauvoir assumed responsibilities from the position of her own relative security that she could not have lived a life without reflecting on and exposing truer accounts of the political events of the French empire. From these self-imposed ethical constraints, Beauvoir became involved in the legal case of Djamila Boupacha. By feeling responsibility for French citizens' resistance against ending colonialism in Algeria, Beauvoir decided to act by participating in the liberation of Djamila Boupacha, whose freedom and life depended on the decrees of the French government.

As Julien Murphy notes in "Beauvoir and the Algerian War: Toward a Postcolonial Ethics," the Algerian War and Boupacha's imprisonment inspired Beauvoir to change her position on the real possibility of the women's freedom. Her efforts to make Boupacha's case known to the public as a means of gaining international recognition of the injustices of Boupacha's imprisonment by the French colonial administration enabled Beauvoir interactively and concretely to form a more nuanced conception of freedom than those elucidated in *The Ethics of Ambiguity*.[44] Moreover, as Ursula Tidd notes, Beauvoir "was involved in meetings to support the FLN and gave talks supporting an independent Algeria. She [also] defended a former Rouen student, Jacqueline Guerroudj, now a teacher in Algeria and involved with the Armée de Liberation Nationale, and managed to save her from execution."[45] Beauvoir's introduction to the book *Djamila Boupacha*, her news articles, and deliberations in her publication *Force of Circumstance* illustrate how her resolve against the colonial system incited her to action and resistance. Unlike her earlier writings on the condition of non-Europeans, as featured in *America Day by Day*, Beauvoir did not conceive of the situation of Algerian women under the French colonial system as synonymous with a caste system. In *America Day by Day*, she problematically concluded that Black Americans were ultimately doomed to a state of despair and oppression. In other words, while Beauvoir could foresee a change in the political freedom of Algerians after the war, she was unable to foresee any political freedom for Black Americans after desegregation. This is why Beauvoir argued that Black Americans were more of a caste in comparison to the Algerians.

My analysis of Beauvoir is not intended solely to show that when she began to speak up about colonialism, she had an anti-colonialist and anti-racist agenda, as this has already been demonstrated by Margaret Simons in, for example, her article "Beauvoir and the Problem of Racism," featured in *Philosophers on Race*.[46] Rather, I incorporate the works of Beauvoir into my analysis of the French colonial system after the Second World War, in order to show her contribution to the situation of White women, or colonizer women, and of non-White women or colonized women. What I aim to represent in this book is that women were not passive subjects of the French colonial system because, as Beauvoir's philosophical reflections indicate, women deliberated about their oppression and racial privilege in the first person and, like Beauvoir, colonialism consumed their very thoughts and beings. I now begin the body of the book.

NOTES

1. Simons, *Beauvoir and The Second Sex*, 66, 170–71, 181.

2. Gines, "Sartre, Beauvoir, and the Race," 35.

3. Kathryn T. Gines, "Comparative and Competing Frameworks of Oppression in Simone de Beauvoir's *The Second Sex*," *Graduate Faculty Philosophy Journal* 35, no. 1–2 (2014): 251–73.

4. Ibid., 261–65.

5. Laura Hengehold and Nancy Bauer, *A Companion to Simone de Beauvoir* (Hoboken, NJ: John Wiley & Sons, 2017).

6. Mary Mary Caputi, "Beauvoir and the Case of Djamila Boupacha," in *Simone de Beauvoir's Political Thinking*, ed. Lori Jo Marso and Patricia Moynagh (Chicago, IL: University of Illinois Press, 2006), 121.

7. Simone de Beauvoir, *Force of Circumstance, Vol. 2 : Hard Times, 1952-1962* (New York, NY: Paragon House, 1992), 221–28.

8. Jean-Paul Sartre, *Colonialism and Neocolonialism* (New York, NY: Routledge, 2006), 38.

9. Frantz Fanon, *Black Skin, White Masks* (New York, NY: Grove Press, 1967), 112.

10. It is only in 1962 that Algerian women acquired the right to vote.

11. Sartre, *Colonialism and Neocolonialism*, 49, 52.

12. See, for example, Carole Pateman, *The Sexual Contract* (Stanford, CA: Stanford University Press, 1988), 4–5. Pateman examines this reality and its implications for gender and power relations.

13. Jean-Paul Sartre, *Life Situations: Essays Written and Spoken* (New York, NY: Pantheon Books, 1977), 93.

14. Ibid., 94.

15. Fanon, *Black Skin*, 41–82.

16. T. Sharpley-Whiting, *Frantz Fanon: Conflicts and Feminisms* (Lanham, MD: Rowman & Littlefield, 1998), 9–16.

17. Fanon, *Black Skin*, 18, 112; Frantz Fanon, *The Wretched of the Earth Frantz Fanon*. Translated from the French by Richard Philcox. Introductions by Jean-Paul Sartre and Homi K. Bhabha (New York, NY: Grove Press, 2004), 8, 11, 13, 22, 25.

18. Reiland Rabaka, *Forms of Fanonism : Frantz Fanon's Critical Theory and the Dialectics of Decolonization* (Lanham, MD: Lexington Books, 2010), 99.

19. Ibid., 99–100.

20. Fanon, *Black Skin*, 117.

21. Beatrice Stith Clark, "Forward," in *Mayotte Capécia, I Am a Martinican Woman & The White Negress : Two Novelettes* (Pueblo, CO: Passeggiata Press, 1997), xi.

22. Fanon, *Black Skin*, 47–48.

23. Ibid., 47, 59–60.

24. Ibid., 42.

25. Sharpley-Whiting, *Frantz Fanon*, 10.

26. Christiane Makward, *Mayotte Capécia, Ou, L'aliénation Selon Fanon* (Paris: Editions Karthala, 1999), 21. Makward's research suggests that Fanon did not do a critical assessment of women of color.

27. Anthony Alessandrini, *Frantz Fanon : Critical Perspectives* (New York, NY: Routledge, 1999), 45. Rey Chow, "The Politics of Admittance: Female Sexual Agency, Miscegenation, and the Formation of Community," in *Frantz Fanon: Critical Perspectives*, ed. Anthony C. Alessandrini (New York, NY: Routledge, 1999), 45. Chow's analysis suggests that Fanon examined the sexual agency of women of color as a means separating them of black alienation.

28. Sharpley-Whiting, *Frantz Fanon*, 11.

29. Alessandrini, *Frantz Fanon*, 38.

30. Sharpley-Whiting, *Frantz Fanon*, 36.

31. Ibid.

32. Fanon, *Black Skin*, 64–65.

33. Ibid.

34. T. Sharpley-Whiting, *Negritude Women* (Minneapolis, MN: University of Minnesota Press, 2002), 16–24.

35. Emily Kirkland and McTighe Musil, "La Marianne Noire" (PhD diss., UCLA, 2007); C. Nigel Gibson, *Rethinking Fanon* (New York, NY: Humanity Books, 1999), 285.

36. Traci C. West, "Extending Black Feminist Sisterhood in the Face of Violence," *Convergences: Black Feminism and Continental Philosophy* (Albany, NY: SUNY Press, 2010), 160. West suggests that Fanon's descriptions of the sexual encounters

between White women and men of color are solely for the purpose of self-serving men of color. In this sense, Fanon perpetuates the objectification of White women as sexual objects of men's desire, and therefore subtracts any agency White women have in such interpersonal relations.

37. Valerie Amos and Pratibha Parmar, "Challenging Imperial Feminism," *Feminist Review*, no. 80 (January 1, 2005): 49.

38. Sonia Kruks, "Simone de Beauvoir and the Politics of Privilege," *Hypatia* 20, no. 1 (2005): 186.

39. Ibid.

40. Sonia Kruks, *Simone de Beauvoir and the Politics of Ambiguity*. Studies in Feminist Philosophy (New York, NY: Oxford University Press, 2012), 93–95.

41. Beauvoir, *Force of Circumstance*, 87.

42. Ibid.

43. Ibid.

44. J. Murphy, "Beauvoir and the Algerian War: Toward a Postcolonial Ethics," in *Feminist Interpretations of Simone de Beauvoir* (University Park, PA: Penn State University Press, 1995), 264–65.

45. Ursula Tidd, *Simone De Beauvoir* (London: Reaktion Books, 2009), 122.

46. Julie K. Ward and Tommy L. Lott, *Philosophers on Race: Critical Essays* (Malden, MA: Blackwell, 2002), 261–83.

Part II

FIRST PHILOSOPHY, FREEDOM, AND GENDER IDENTITY

Chapter 2

The Second Sex

Beauvoir's First Famous Colonial Text

FRAMING *THE SECOND SEX*

In *The Second Sex* (and *The Ethics of Ambiguity* [*1947*]), published in 1949, Beauvoir references French colonialism[1] in her analysis of oppression—gender oppression, in particular. Beauvoir's notes on gender oppressions in the French colonial system actually enabled her to elaborate on the situation of White women in France. In other words, Beauvoir used the condition of the colonized to further reflect on the condition of White women.[2] To Beauvoir, while the oppressive measures of the colonist—in particular the male colonial administrator—could cease with the end of the colonial system, the system of gender oppression is not as easy to dissolve.[3] Relating the colonial system more to a system of political oppression than to a specific system of racial oppression, as Sartre did, Beauvoir claims that gender oppression is a more permanent, fundamental, and long-standing apparatus than colonial oppression in the French empire. Beauvoir prioritizes gender oppression above colonial oppression and demonstrates precisely how the former overarches the latter, thereby using the condition of the colonized to elaborate on the political and interpersonal conditions of White women. From this angle, Beauvoir's appropriation of colonial oppression to shed light on gender oppression betrays unintentional biases; she cannot fathom that the struggles and sufferings of the colonized cannot inevitably be compared to the oppression of colonizer women. Instead, racism and sexism work hand in hand in the condition of the oppressed; neither racism nor sexism subsumes the other.

COLONIZER WOMEN AS THE OTHER
IN BEAUVOIR'S PHILOSOPHY

To illustrate her point on the relation between gender oppression and colonial oppression, Beauvoir draws on the situation of Black people. Beauvoir alludes to the ways French colonialists created the caricature of the Black man as thievish, lazy, and deceitful in order to racially discriminate against them.[4] According to Beauvoir, the caricature that French colonialists created for White women resulted in a more fundamental oppression, in that, unlike Black men who did not take the racial stereotypes of French colonialists as a reflection of their identity, White women assumed the gender stereotypes of the French colonialists as a reflection of their femininity.[5] The difference between the situation of Black men and White women's response to the stereotypes of French colonialist, then, shows the permanent effects of the traditional order of patriarchy upon the situation of women in the Western world. To Beauvoir, Black men, even if they had to accept these stereotypes, as in the case of Black slaves,[6] knew that they were being stereotyped, whereas women generally did not realize that they were being stereotyped. White women respectfully obeyed the social dictates of stereotypes, an observation that led Beauvoir to conclude that the lot of White women was even worse than that of Black slaves and colonial natives.[7] White women rarely questioned the sexist ideologies White men associated with their feminine identities. Indeed, to Beauvoir these women took the sexist ideologies behind the gender stereotypes enforced by White men only as a positive reflection of Western female gender traditions and of their femininity.

Already, in her description of the colonial context of France, Beauvoir associates racial oppression with the condition of Black men and gender oppression with the condition of White women. "French colonialists" or "French administrators"[8] were intended by Beauvoir to designate French men. By explicitly equating French colonialists and French men, Beauvoir casts French women as the oppressed, not the oppressors. A limit, then, in Beauvoir's analysis of French women in the 1940s is that she does not grant them any part as oppressors. As such, Beauvoir fails to consider, for example, the ways that French colonizer women both contributed to the stereotypes made about Black men, while wholly ignoring the specific plights of Black women.

Beauvoir's attempt to relate racial oppression with Black men and gender oppression with White women is a particularly fraught issue in *The Second Sex*. This categorization limits what Beauvoir's writings on gender oppression from the 1940s can offer to the racial and gender oppression of Black women, for example. Beauvoir's race/gender analogy problematizes any analytical context that would explicitly take into account the situation of colonized women. Simply stated, as Kathryn Gines explains in her article "Sartre,

Beauvoir, and the Race/Gender Analogy," the race/gender analogy is the use of racial oppression as an analogy for gender oppression.[9] One shortcoming of this equation is that it tends to emphasize the situation of Black men and White women while ignoring or wholly negating the situation of women of color.[10] Another flaw in this analogy is that it is frequently exploited to support members of groups and their causes even when those groups are often themselves participating in or complicit with some form of anti-Black racism.[11] Further, Beauvoir's analysis is unintentionally racist, failing as it does to acknowledge that Black women are confronted by both a "woman question" and a race problem simultaneously.[12] This intersectionality is lost on Beauvoir's analysis. When it comes to comparing slavery to gender oppression, Beauvoir misses the opportunity to account for the situation of Black female slaves, whose experiences may offer more comparable points in Beauvoir's analysis on the gender oppression of White women. Moreover, although Beauvoir's analysis of gender oppression from the 1940s alludes to non-European women in classical antiquity, for example, as her analysis of Jewish and Arab women shows,[13] she makes no reference to the circumstances of non-European women within the French colonial context. What we see more in *The Second Sex* is Beauvoir's attempt to examine the situation of French women, such as herself, within the patriarchal history of France and the history of Western norms and knowledge.

Because I find it important to discuss the situation of colonizer women within the French empire and because Beauvoir briefly discusses the context of colonialism in *The Ethics of Ambiguity*, I will supplement my discussion with material from Beauvoir's analysis of colonialism in *The Ethics of Ambiguity*. Beauvoir's feminist philosophy is primarily based on the situations of French White women and the political climate of the 1940s, which enabled them to acquire more rights in the public sector, such as the ability to work outside the home and the right to vote. As such, the term "women" as used in this chapter and, indeed, as drawn from Beauvoir primarily stands for the conditions of White women living in the French empire after the Second World War.

To begin, as she observes in *The Second Sex*, the French Revolution did not change the situation of women in France.[14] In *A New Dawn for the Second Sex: Women's Freedom Practices in World Perspective,* Karen Vintges presents a similar observation on the situation of women, as I will claim below.[15] The difference between my analysis on freedom and women in the thoughts of Beauvoir and that of Vintges is that I claim Beauvoir's reflections are more appropriate for discussing the situation of women in the French empire than the situation of any other national group of women. After the French Revolution, women were still oppressed and subordinate to men. To this point, the universal suffrage that the male population acquired through the Declaration of Rights of Man was not extended to French women. The "enlightened elites,"[16] or "middle-class men,"[17] as Beauvoir calls them in *The Ethics of Ambiguity*, were opposed "to the extension of universal suffrage by adducing the incompetence of the masses, of [French] women, of the natives [men and women] in the colonies."[18] Aligning the condition of French women to that of French colonized subjects and claiming neither French women nor colonized were educated or fit to vote allowed French middle-class men to deny the right to vote to these members of French empire, Beauvoir explains. Middle-class men made women and the colonized politically not free. Though I will discuss Beauvoir's analysis of voting rights among the colonized and White women in further detail later, I however briefly take up this issue here because it is in terms of liberal political rights that Beauvoir in part discusses the social and political oppression of colonized and White women. So with her analysis of liberal political rights, Beauvoir seeks to show how the colonized and White women are disenfranchised. As Beauvoir explains in *The Ethics of Ambiguity*, "all oppressive regimes become stronger through the degradation of the oppressed."[19] As was the case for Arabs in Algeria and women in France, denying their worthiness to vote denigrated them to a position in reality that was comparable to the imagined perceptions the French administrators had of these members of the French empire.

Moreover, to Beauvoir, the claim on the part of middle-class men that neither French women nor the colonized could vote was based on the assumption that these members of the French empire were incapable to rule.[20] Yet, as she argues, making French women and the colonized eligible to vote did not necessarily predestine these members of the French empire to govern and participate in creating laws in France. Granting the right to vote to French women and the colonized, unlike the privileges it granted French men, would not have equaled a decision to let them govern.[21] Instead, the decision of granting the right to vote to French women and the colonized only further reflected the limitations and inconsistencies that these members of the French empire experienced within their acquired social, economic, and political rights. In other words, granting the right to vote to French women and the colonized only showed that these members of the French empire did not have the same right as White French middle-class men despite the fact that their political freedom was not the same as White French middle-class men. Despite being granted the right to vote, French women and the colonized did not have and could not do what White French middle class had and could do. The right to vote granted to White women and the colonized virtually had no bearing on the governance and decision-making within the French government. For example, although "women first held ministerial positions in the late 1930s, before they were even allowed to vote, the number of women ministers remained negligible for decades after women became part of the electorate."[22]

Specifically, in the chapter titled "The Independent Woman," from *The Second Sex*, Beauvoir examines the overlooked social, economic, and political constraints that French women faced in the aftermath of acquiring the right to vote in 1944. The legal measure that gave women the right to vote in France was signed into law on April 21, 1944, under a provisional government led by General Charles de Gaulle, then based in Algiers, women in France only cast their first ballot on April, 29, 1945, in what were France first general elections since the country stop being under German Occupation. The order established that women are eligible voters and under the same terms as men. I take note of French women acquiring the right to vote in 1944—unlike American women, who acquired the right to vote in 1920—because it points to a pivotal moment in the Beauvoir's feminist philosophy since speaking about the right to vote in the 1940s clearly indicates her readership. In other words, *The Second Sex* seeks to explain the conditions of White French women during the 1940s for White French women during the 1940s. As Gail Weis notes, Beauvoir endeavors to show the multiple ways women experience oppression.[23] I would add that her analysis also sheds light on the ways women understand their subjectivity.

Even with the right to vote, Beauvoir argues, women exist in a condition of vassalage.[24] That women were granted the right to vote did not necessarily affect the infrastructure of French society.[25] The right to vote did not make the rights of women symmetrical to the rights of men. In claiming to enfranchise women through humanist law, the French man attempted to describe and justify women's oppression with a description of himself, of his theories, and histories of humanity.[26] Granting women the right to vote by virtue of humanist principles, as Sara Heinämaa suggests, further subdues a cohesive examination of the oppression of women,[27] due to the reality that women's relationships to the history of politics have been different from that of men.[28] By granting women the right, further inquiry into the oppression of women was halted. Once the vote was granted, it was assumed the "job was done" so to speak. As Carole Pateman has shown in *The Sexual Contract*, liberal political theories did not view women as the subject of political discourse, which meant that women were excluded from the original political contract.[29] To Pateman, women's exclusion means that the political discourse itself primarily reflects the interests of men rather than women. In view of the history of women and politics, granting women the right to vote perpetuates myths, as Judith Okely states, about "women's objective subordination and oppression."[30]

To evince an aspect of women's oppression unaddressed by universal suffrage, Beauvoir centers her analysis on the persistence of economic disenfranchisement, in terms of job opportunities and pay alone, among the majority of women in France. Writing *The Second Sex* during the mid- to late 1940s, Beauvoir observes that, while it is the case that each woman citizen has the right to vote, "these civil liberties remain theoretical as long as they are unaccompanied by economic freedom."[31] This economic disenfranchisement reveals granting the right to vote to be a paltry effort; if women are not financially independent, the liberal political rights they are acquiring will not render their situation symmetrical to that of men. In economic terms, women, unlike men, were politically and socially restricted.

Here Beauvoir suggests that it is in fact wage labor and financial independence that can put the liberty of women to practice.[32] The woman, she describes, "when she is productive, active, . . . in her projects she concretely affirms her status as subject; in connection with the aims she pursues, with the money and the rights she takes possession of, she makes trial of and senses her responsibility."[33] In describing what women ought to strive for—education, money, freedom, and responsibility, Beauvoir alludes to the legacy of women's unpaid labor, primarily practiced in households, which made them responsible for the care and well-being of others as well as financially dependent on their husbands. The title to property rights under political liberalism, as shown in the works of John Locke, means that what a man works for ought to belong to him.[34] Housework denied women a title to private property. Through housework, women, in general, owned nothing and, as such, they were denied autonomy and personal responsibility.

Writing about Beauvoir's work, Toril Moi argues that the chapter in *The Second Sex* on the independent woman suggests, "as long as women are prevented from earning their own living, they will always be dependent on others."[35] Being an independent woman assumes the material condition of earning a living. More specifically, it is the paid work that women do in the public sphere and not in the household (the private sphere) that can grant women title to a liberal political identity, which, as Carole Pateman explains, is made upon a person's place within the sphere of civil society.[36] From the perspective of liberal political theories—propounded in the work of Hobbes, Locke, and Rousseau—civil society is divided into the public sphere and the private sphere. But, as Pateman shows, the division of civil society into the public sphere and the private sphere reflected the order of sexual political difference between the rights of men and the rights of women.[37] Establishing the function of the public/private divide within liberal political theories asserts that "the private sphere is typically presupposed as a necessary, naturalized foundation for civil, i.e., public life, but treated as irrelevant to the concerns of political theories and political activities."[38] Given that the private sphere is part of civil society but separated from the public or civil sphere, it follows that a person could only gain liberal political identity through the exercise of activities in the public sphere.

Furthermore, given the sexual political order of liberal political theories, both men and women had rights to the private sphere, rights to a life in the household, but only men had rights to a life in the public sphere. Traditionally, then, men were the only ones who had rights to civil liberty, and their liberties were considered the relevant concerns that would establish civil society. In being barred from the public sphere, women neither gained title to a liberal political identity nor influence the establishment of liberal political rights through their lives within households. Politically, the lives of women within the households could never grant women a sense of self-sovereignty. So, in urging women to become economically independent, Beauvoir is actually urging women to take part in the civil sphere or (public sphere), in the hope that their participation in the economy would alter not only the subject position of women, but also the infrastructure or basic institutions of France.

However, Beauvoir became pessimistic about the participation of women in the public sphere and settled on the reality that the infrastructure or basic institutions of the French liberal political system could not be easily changed. As such, Beauvoir complicated her position on women's economic enfranchisement, asserting, "It is not to be supposed, however, that the mere combination of the right to vote and a job constitutes a complete emancipation: working, today, is not liberty."[39] Given the deeply entrenched subordinate status of women in French society, and the infrastructure of the French liberal political system, earning a wage along with having the right to vote did not necessarily free women. As Nancy J. Hirschmann shows, if women enter the workforce from the social liberal perspective that they are inferior to men, the market will ensure their failure.[40] The assumptions that society makes about women will affect their performance—and, importantly, the wages they receive—in the workforce. Women's assumptions about themselves will affect their performance too.

Toril Moi presents a stronger interpretation than Nancy J. Hirschmann of Beauvoir's chapter on the independent woman, arguing that independent women are not free.[41] To Toril Moi, independent women are not free precisely because "women actually seeking paid work . . . are confronted with class exploitation and sexist oppression at every turn."[42] The classism and sexism built into the infrastructure of the French liberal political and economic structures perpetuate the subordination of independent women, glossing over inconsistencies within conceptions of women's liberty. As Beauvoir explains, once women join the workforce, they take on the lot of the majority of male working-class workers—themselves exploited under capitalism.[43] Furthermore, "the social structure has not been much modified by the changes in women's condition; this world always belonged to men, still retains the form they have given it."[44] Because the French system is built upon the ideals, theories, and histories of men, that women were granted the right to vote and to earn wages does not necessarily affect French social and political structures.

The classism and sexism that independent women routinely encounter reflect the irresolvable conflict, as Sonia Kruks shows, that these women face when seeking "human freedom"[45] from the purview of their feminine destiny. To Beauvoir, the feminine destiny, which means constructing an identity that reaffirms women's dependence on others because of their sex—indeed, to construct an infantilized identity[46]—poses a conundrum for the notion of an independent human individual.[47] The advantages, she says, "man enjoys, which makes itself felt from his childhood, is that his vocation as a human being in no way runs counter to his destiny as a male."[48] When a man becomes independent, he engages himself in the project of man, thus fulfilling his destiny. When a woman becomes independent, she has to reject her destiny. A man is unlike a woman because, in becoming independent, he is not divided.[49] In becoming independent, women have to renounce part, if not all, of their femininity. But Beauvoir states, in essentialist terms, that "to renounce her femininity is to renounce a part of her humanity."[50] Given the state of history and politics, women could not take part in human freedom without following their feminine destiny. Women occupy a marginalized identity in the first place such that they by necessity have to participate in the project of human freedom. That the feminine destiny implies a historicized and politicized state of subordination means that "wom[e]n's oppression cannot be overcome except within the framework of the fuller abolition of human oppression."[51] The gender category intersects with all other marginalized identities. To overcome the oppression of women, we must also overcome racism, classism, and so on. So, for example, in order to consider the economic disenfranchisement of women in France and women's lack of economic freedom in France, the economic oppression of working-class men should also be examined.

Following the interpretation supported by Kruks might prevent us from assuming that to have the right to human freedom and to be independent necessarily implies that women ought to follow the destiny of men. For the purpose of my study, to be independent does not necessarily imply that one ought to follow the destiny of White men. While the right to vote and earning a living might enable women to maneuver within the capitalist French liberal political system, only when women's descriptions, theories, and histories are equitably integrated into the development of France's infrastructure can the legacy of women's subordination potentially alter the power dynamic between genders. Examining both the political and the economic predominance of French men over French women can only provide us with some justification for the liberation of French women. To Beauvoir, in particular, the gender and sexual predominance of French men over French women must also be contested.

CONCLUSION

To Beauvoir, colonizer women were oppressed. The meager political rights they acquired during French colonial rule, such as the right to vote, further revealed the problems and contradictions of their gender, which was built upon the social and political status of being subordinate to French men. Beauvoir's comparison between Black "male" slaves and White French women failed because it negated the position of Black "female" slaves; her comparison between the lack of rights of the colonized—both men and women, and White colonizer women—is less apt to criticism. In France's history, colonized women like colonizer women received the right to vote well after their male counterparts. In France's history, men colonizers privileged their rights over the rights of White women and the colonized. Taking note of this context in Beauvoir's analysis illuminates how, at once, her thoughts went awry, and her thoughts led to fruitful analysis. I propose that Beauvoir's analysis on the inter-subjectivity of the colonized and White is progressive, while her lack of awareness about gender and racial intersectionality leaves itself open to strong criticism. And so, what would be the goal of embracing *The Second Sex* if Beauvoir denies women's presence on one side but acknowledges women on the other? Certainly, we must read *The Second Sex* as a text of its own historical moment. As Beauvoir scholars are well-aware, the French feminist read Mary Wollstonecraft, Virginia Woolf, the French suffragettes, and Richard Wright; however, she was unaware of Ida B. Wells or Paulette Nardal.[52] Even if one were to discover that Beauvoir had read the works of both of these Black women, it cannot be said that she understood the dilemma of experiencing both racism and sexism simultaneously. In other words, the importance that she granted to reading Woolf or even Wright, for example, did not entice Beauvoir to seek out stories about the contemporary lived experiences of Black women. When it comes to the situation of Black women and at least in *The Second Sex,* Beauvoir suffered from ignorance, not racism.

NOTES

1. Simone de Beauvoir, *The Second Sex* (New York, NY: Vintage Books, 1989), 598, 723; Simone de Beauvoir, *The Ethics of Ambiguity* (Secaucus, NJ: The Citadel Press, 1972), 101.

2. Beauvoir, *Second Sex*, 598.

3. Ibid., 723.

4. Ibid., 616.

5. Ibid.

6. Ibid., 598.

7. Ibid.

8. Ibid., 723.

9. Gines, "Sartre, Beauvoir, and the Race," 36.

10. Ibid.

11. Ibid.

12. Ibid., 44.

13. Beauvoir, *Second Sex*, 84–85.

14. Ibid., 109.

15. Karen Vintges, *A New Dawn for the Second Sex: Women's Freedom Practices in World Perspective* (Amsterdam: Amsterdam University Press, 2017), 11.

16. Beauvoir, *Ethics of Ambiguity*, 138.

17. Beauvoir, *Second Sex*, 109.

18. Beauvoir, *Ethics of Ambiguity*, 139.

19. Ibid., 101.

20. Ibid., 139.

21. Ibid.

22. Caroline Lambert, "French Women in Politics: The Long Road to Parity," *Brookings* (blog) (November 30, 2001), 2. https://www.brookings.edu/articles/frenc h-women-in-politics-the-long-road-to-parity/

23. Gail Weiss, "Challenging Choices: An Ethic of Oppression," in *The Philosophy of Simone de Beauvoir: Critical Essays*, ed. Margaret Simons (Bloomington, IN: Indiana University Press, 2006), 243.

24. Beauvoir, *Second Sex*, 679.

25. Ibid., 680.

26. Sara Heirnämaa, "Simone de Beauvoir's Phenomenology of Sexual Difference," in *The Philosophy of Simone de Beauvoir: Critical Essays*, ed. Margaret Simons (Bloomington, IN: Indiana University Press, 2006), 32.

27. Heirnämaa, "Simone de Beauvoir's Phenomenology," 32.

28. Máire Fedelma Cross, "Women and Politics," in *Women in Contemporary France*, ed. Abigail Gregory (New York, NY: Berg, 2000), 89.

29. Pateman, *Sexual Contract*, 5.

30. Judith Okely, "Rereading the Second Sex," in *Simone de Beauvoir: A Critical Reader*, ed. Elizabeth Fallaize (New York, NY: Routledge, 1998), 22.

31. Beauvoir, *Second Sex*, 679.

32. Ibid.

33. Ibid., 680.

34. John Locke, *Second Treatise of Government* (Indianapolis, IN: Hackett Pub. Co., 1980), 19.

35. Toril Moi, "Independent Women" and "Narratives of Liberation," in *Simone de Beauvoir: A Critical Reader*, ed. Elizabeth Fallaize (New York, NY: Routledge, 1998), 74.

36. Pateman, *Sexual Contract*, 11.

37. Ibid.

38. Ibid.

39. Beauvoir, *Second Sex*, 681.

40. N. J Hirschmann, *Gender, Class, and Freedom in Modern Political Theory* (Princeton, NJ: Princeton University Press, 2008), 215.

41. Elizabeth Fallaize, *Simone de Beauvoir: A Critical Reader* (London: Routledge, 1998), 75.

42. Ibid., 74.

43. Beauvoir, *Second Sex*, 680.

44. Ibid.

45. Sonia Kruks, "Beauvoir: The Weight of Situation," in *Simone de Beauvoir: A Critical Reader*, ed. Elizabeth Fallaize (New York, NY: Routledge, 1998), 57.

46. Beauvoir, *Ethics of Ambiguity*, 37.

47. Beauvoir, *Second Sex*, 682.

48. Ibid.

49. Ibid.

50. Ibid.

51. Fallaize, *Simone de Beauvoir*, 64.

52. Sanos, *Simone de Beauvoir*, 24–25.

Chapter 3

The Others' Other

Toward an Inter-Subjective Ethics

TRANSITION FROM WHITE WOMEN
TO WOMEN OF COLOR

Given the purpose of my inquiry, which is in part to cover the presence of French female colonized and colonizer subjects in postcolonial philosophy, I now turn to the situation of colonized women. Here, as in the previous section on colonizer women, I focus on the gender and racial oppression, freedom and rights of colonized French female subjects as they relate to Beauvoir's analyses. Specifically, since I intend to do a comparative analysis among the views on freedom of Beauvoir, Sartre, and female French-Martinican writer Paulette Nardal, I focus on the situation of colonized women in Martinique—an overseas department of France.

GENDER OPPRESSION AND THE INTERSUBJECTIVE
RELATIONS AMONG COLONIZED
WOMEN AND COLONIZER WOMEN

To begin, it was only in 1946, two years after French women were granted the right to vote, that Martinique became an overseas department of France and Martinican women were granted the right to vote and to participate in the general French elections.[1] Though a few free Black men had been able to vote since 1848 in the West Indies in general,[2] only in 1870 could the population of Black men vote in French colonial administrative elections.[3] In view of this, the difference in years between Martinican men's right to vote and the right to vote of Martinican women is at least 76 years.

A few places in the West Indies, such as Guadeloupe, nurtured a stronger political activism among women, than the women of Martinique, within the field of governmental politics. As such, that may have offered a place for women who sought professional positions as politicians, as members within the French assembly, and within political parties during the twentieth century.[4] But women in Martinique who had the opportunity to be political expressed their views on the political prospects and freedom of women and of all Martinicans through more literary and sociocultural venues, precisely because the leading women in Martinique who became political were, for the most part, authors by profession.

For example, in 1945, Paulette Nardal, an author and journalist, founded the *Rassemblement Féminin Martiniquais* (The Martinican Women's Assembly), the Martinican branch of *L' Union Féminine Civique et Sociale* (The Women's Civic and Social Union, based in France). This group was formed to urge French-Martinican women to vote for the first time, precisely because French women in France had already voted for the first time on April 29, 1945.[5] Her activism contributed to the 33 percent of women in Martinique who voted for the first time in 1946.[6] As Sharpley-Whiting notes, the *Rassemblement Féminin Martiniquais* enabled Nardal to:

> further the interests of women on the island, particularly as they related to, among other matters, race, social justice and its intersection with women's rights and duties as mothers, workers, citizens and newly enfranchised voters and the colonial hangovers Martinique continued to face even at the dawn of the island's becoming an overseas department of France.[7]

Through her organization—buoyed by her professional status as an author and journalist—Nardal was able to interrogate the political rights of women in Martinique and contribute to their political education.

As such, what we find in an analysis of Nardal is what Beauvoir ignores (as do Fanon and Sartre): specifically, engaging with the political disenfranchisement of Black women. Nardal's contribution to Beauvoir's, Sartre's, and Fanon's politics is to bring the liberal political disenfranchisement and lack of freedom among colonized women into the discussion of French colonialism. Her ideas were discussed *by* Sartre, Beauvoir, and Fanon. However, these intellectuals did not always relate the idea of liberal political disenfranchisement to situation of colonized women. Nardal's contribution affords an opportunity to investigate what women in Martinique contributed throughout the cultural venues that formed when Martinique transitioned from being a colony of France to an overseas department. Martinican women participated in the development of Black and Creole national identity in Martinique. Such an examination puts into context the condition of Black and Creole women as it related to questions concerning the racial condition of people of color in general.

The immediacy "of her calls to voting as part of women's duty is in no small part a function of the newness of enfranchisement."[8] Nardal saw the enfranchisement of women in Martinique as a positive move within the liberal political achievement of women. Unlike Beauvoir, she did not formulate that granting women the right to vote would merely eclipse the realities of women's oppression. Rather, Nardal saw the enfranchisement of women in Martinique as a venue that would give a political voice to women. In other words, Nardal saw the right to vote as a tool, not a factor. Nardal sees the enfranchisement of women as a tool for making *further* progress toward the full emancipation of women rather than treating enfranchisement as if it were the *end* of all sexist oppression.

Nardal explains in "From an Electoral Point of View" that women bring to political actions, such as the act of voting, a fresh strength and insight that comes from their daily connections to the concrete realities of life.[9] On this account, for example, women's work in the household influences how they view their liberal political rights. The specific situations that women have experienced enable them to contribute effectively to society through the vote. Although Nardal supports Beauvoir's thesis that the situation of women as women has marginalized their political status, she goes beyond Beauvoir's thesis by claiming that it is just such a situation that also grants women an advantage in politics. In the scope of Martinican women's history, Nardal wrote and created social and literary organizations that advocated political actions among women. Subject to French imperial control—and in comparison, to French women—women of color had seen very little political, economic, and social improvement to their condition. Nardal felt that her call to political action was just as important as her writing, which challenged the gender and racial discrimination experienced by women citizens of Martinique.[10]

Nardal supported Sartre's conception of freedom, which posits that one's freedom is dependent upon the sense of responsibility we have for others when we act—the sense of responsibility simply the result or expression of our freedom.[11] She did not embrace Beauvoir's claims about freedom, expressed in *The Second Sex* and *The Ethics of Ambiguity*, which proposes that the concrete constraints of our situations (e.g., the concept of women and the concept of the feminine) and physical embodiment (e.g., the female body and female experiences) limited women's freedom.[12] Sartre's model of freedom, which endorses interconnections among freedom, choice, and responsibility, was much more appealing to Nardal. Sartre's conception of freedom, similar to Nardal's, provides more autonomy to people marginalized by liberalism and from both of their conception of freedom; even through oppression, the oppressed can act. This perspective on freedom, enabled Nardal to fight for the women's suffrage in Martinique. As Robert Bernasconi shows, to Sartre, "Existentialism's first move is to make every man aware of what he is and to make the full responsibility of his existence rest on him. And when we say that a man is responsible for himself, we do not only mean that he is responsible for his own individuality, but that he is responsible for all men."[13] According to Sartre, man's choice bears a sense of responsibility that bridges the gap between himself and all other men. In coming to terms with the responsibility that man has for all men, he will be able to act freely within the concrete circumstances of mankind.[14] For Sartre, our freedom carries responsibility for the sake of all others. In this respect, Nardal's choice to urge Martinican women to vote, and the choice to support women's suffrage in Martinique, shows the degree to which her freedom was determined by the concrete circumstances of all people—not just Martinican women.

However, Nardal diverged from Sartre's position on freedom by claiming that women in Martinique, herself included, would be the ones to benefit the most from the enfranchisement of Martinican women. In other words, while Nardal may have supported the sense of universal responsibility built into Sartre's conception of freedom, she agreed less about the degree to which the choice she made on the behalf of the rights of Martinican women affected everyone. To Nardal, at the very most, apart from Martinican women themselves, the French women from *L'Union Féminine Civique et Sociale* would be more concerned with establishing women's suffrage in Martinique precisely because they had assisted Nardal in building a branch of their organization there. From this perspective, then, we can gather that the self-interested parties for whose concrete circumstances we act make us responsible for ourselves. Only when we are directly connected to the circumstances within sociopolitical events that we feel responsible as to how our actions affect aftermath of circumstances.

In other words, it is through some, and not everyone, that we come to be responsible for ourselves. We come to *recognize* our responsibility for ourselves through certain others. Sartre's philosophy suggests that individual freedom is influenced by the concrete circumstances of all. Yet, the singularity of the concrete circumstances of all becomes universalized, such that actions made on the behalf of a single group of women do inevitably affect the condition of all men and women in general. Through Sartre's universal conception of freedom, or conception of everyone's freedom, the specific situation of each person merges with the individual sense of responsibility for all men.

To Beauvoir, on the other hand, a person's situation—not the person's sense of responsibility for all and the person's choices—determines the freedom of such a person. As Sonia Kruks recounts, Beauvoir's objection to Sartre's concept of freedom was based on the problems she saw in the relation of situation to freedom.[15] As Beauvoir argued, Sartre's rules, with which he defined individual freedom in all concrete circumstances, could not always apply to the situation of every person. Specifically examining the situation of women, Beauvoir shows that not everybody in every concrete circumstance is responsible, either for him- or herself or for others. In view of this position, then, contrary to Sartre's analysis suggesting that Nardal urged women in Martinique to vote because she felt that not granting the right to vote to women created inequalities within the establishment of the universal suffrage in the French empire; and contrary to Nardal's own position that urging women in Martinique to vote would benefit women in Martinique— and even some women in France—Beauvoir would argue that Nardal was forced to incite women in Martinique to vote because a good number of these women were not responsible enough to want to vote on their own. Beauvoir maintained that Nardal was responsible for instilling into Martinican women the desire to vote. From this perspective, then, Nardal acted on behalf of other Martinican women precisely because the material and social context of their situations, unlike her own, constrained them from choosing to vote. The average Martinican women did not have the same education and public work experience as Nardal. From Beauvoir's perspective, a concrete examination of the circumstances of individuals—and the circumstances of women in particular—reveals that the concrete circumstances of some people are devoid of freedom.[16] In *The Second Sex*, Beauvoir concludes that, despite the political context that women's suffrage created for women in France, not all women, given their particular situations, knew how to vote. In *The Ethics of Ambiguity*, Beauvoir questions a young woman who criticized the establishment of voting rights for women in France, ignorantly assuming that women would vote according to their own feminine interests if they were granted the right to vote.[17] To Beauvoir, such an assumption could be made only if the young woman believed that the situations of all women were equal. Beauvoir reflects that not every women would even vote—and that not every woman has the same resources to inspire her to vote out of self-interest.

As Kristana Arp notes, in terms of existentialist philosophy, Beauvoir presented a distinct theory of freedom based more on moral freedom than on ontological freedom, the type of freedom that Sartre emphasizes in *Being and Nothingness*, the freedom that all humans possess.[18] Human freedom, according to *Being and Nothingness*, is the ability of consciousness to transcend its material situation. It is "ontological," in the sense that no normal human being cannot fail to be freedom, that Sartre considers that human freedom consists in the ability of consciousness to escape the present. Not only is Beauvoir's moral freedom different from Sartre's ontological freedom, but it also differs from her conception of power, which, to her, means freedom from material and social constraints.[19] According to Arp, Beauvoir's concept of freedom "is the conscious affirmation of one's ontological freedom. And it can only be developed in the absence of certain constraints."[20] Arp attempts to show that Beauvoir's concept of freedom was formulated within the context of material and social constraints, whereby developing moral freedom required assuming a certain sort of relation to other people.[21]

Given that Nardal was involved with French feminist associations, such as *L'Union Féminine Civique et Sociale,* which examined the condition of women and promoted the emancipation of women in French territories,[22] and that such involvement led Nardal to create her own organization for women in Martinique, the juxtaposition of Nardal's analysis of women to Beauvoir's is more feasible, in part because both women, while from different generations,[23] were concerned about the general condition of women within the French patriarchal political and social establishment.

Specifically, in *The Ethics of Ambiguity,* concerned with how specific social situations and the Other shape our subjectivity as well as restrict the possible self-interested choices—moral choices—individual people can make, Beauvoir draws in part on the condition of women to inform her analysis. Primarily because Beauvoir essentializes the condition of women as resembling a childlike state, she limits the choices a woman can make within the confines of her social situation.[24] In other words, given this submissive state of women, it is debatable whether women are even capable of making a moral choice that signals the self-interestedness of liberating themselves. Across civilizations women have been infantilized, unable to author the rules of the societies in which they grow up.

Beauvoir narrows the scope of her analysis to specifically discuss how women's actions affect the ways they are treated as grown-up children in Western countries. Even in contemporary Western countries, she argues:

> Among women who have not had in their work an apprenticeship of freedom, there are still many who take shelter in the shadow of men; they adopt without discussion the opinions and values recognized by their husband or their lover, and that allows them to develop childish qualities which are forbidden to adults because they are based on a feeling of irresponsibility.[25]

In Western countries, similar to the situation of women from non-Western origins, such Asian, African, Arab, and Jewish women, many women have not been educated on their freedom or the possible choices that are available to them and, through their relations with husbands and lovers, become infantilized and, therefore, irresponsible. Ultimately, from Beauvoir's perspective, the majority of women, regardless of their origins or political circumstances—and such was the case with colonized women—were more destined to a state that lacked freedom than a state of freedom.

According to Arp, Beauvoir distinguishes, for example, between the case of the modern Western woman and the African woman or harem slave of the past (women from other civilizations). There exists a "possibility of liberation" for the Western woman, but there is not such a possibility for these other women. The difference lies in the knowledge about their situation available to each.[26] The more aware one is of one's situation through education, the more she is able to transcend her oppression as a woman. According to Beauvoir, then, what the situation of the African woman or harem slave lacks but which exists for Western women is the capacity to educate oneself about one's social subordination. But many European women surely didn't have the means to educate themselves, and many African women surely understood that there are other possibilities than slavery. In appealing to the judgment of the African or harem slave, Beauvoir claims that these women lacked the instrument that could set them free.[27] Persons such as the African or harem slave, as Arp notes in relation to Beauvoir's ethics, "are not able to realize their moral freedom because they are cut off from creating their own future by their oppressors."[28] They have no access to the knowledge and tools that would make them moral free agents, which would enable them to participate in the creation of their future. It's important to be clear about what the claim is—it's that the women couldn't be morally free because they didn't *know* that moral freedom is a possibility for them and also that they simply couldn't become morally free because there were men and legal structures (etc.) who were stopping them from being morally free.

That Beauvoir does not recognize moral freedom in the condition of the harem slave does not mean that the harem slave lacks ontological freedom. Contrary to Beauvoir's assumption and analysis of freedom, the harem slave, like the women in Western society, has ontological freedom—she can act and can make choices within the scope of her situation. The difference, then, is the degree to which the actions and choices of the concubine will change her situation and give her more political freedom in order to free herself from slavery.

However, given Beauvoir's analysis of contemporary Western women, she does not seem to believe they always have the identity that could set them free either.[29] So, in showing doubt about women's capabilities to make moral choices, Beauvoir doubts women's sense of moral freedom—whether they have capacity for freedom, choice, and responsibility. In relating the condition of women to children, her analysis seems to suggest that the state of childhood is devoid of any sense of self and social responsibility. And because women, in general, are devoid of social responsibility, it is debatable, to Beauvoir, whether women are astute enough to, first, recognize their status as "grown-up children" and then act to free themselves from such bondage. To Beauvoir, apart from Western women of today, who are in the "apprenticeship of freedom," or educated to become self-assertive, the condition of women that she describes is applicable to Western women and women of other civilizations. In sum, Beauvoir's position of the freedom of women suggests a de-habilitating standpoint from which women could do very little about their individual situation, in that being denied the ability to develop moral freedom, women cannot necessarily be assigned a moral status.[30]

Beauvoir's position on the freedom of women was contrary to that of Nardal. From Nardal's perspective, as a situated subject, the woman of color could not be free if she could not act with responsibility beyond her situation—in which she experiences racism, sexism, and classism. To accept the reality that liberal political rights were designed beyond the reach of the women of color and not do anything about this would be highly problematic for Nardal. She argues that women of color had a moral identity, and precisely because of the context of their moral status, they had the social duty to participate in their own freedom.[31]

The problem, Arp argues, is that "Beauvoir's ethics hinges on the connection she makes between morality and freedom. If the oppressed lack moral freedom, the implication is that they somehow are not fully moral."[32] From this perspective, Nardal's work becomes invaluable. From Beauvoir's analysis of moral freedom, a conception of the good cannot necessarily be conceived from the gender and racial oppression of colonized women precisely because these women are an oppressed group. Yet Nardal's intellectual trajectory shows that she attempts to present a conception that social and political good can be acquired through the moral status of colonized women; or, of French-Martinican women in particular.

Nardal's conception of freedom recognized the racial and gender constraints of her situation as a woman. Contrarily, to Beauvoir, in *The Ethics of Ambiguity* and also in *The Second Sex*, women's social and physical constraints limited their freedom. As Sharpley-Whiting notes:

> If for Beauvoir, woman has always been cast as man's "Other" and *The Second Sex* endeavors to uncover just what that "Otherness" means for woman, Nardal takes this "Otherness" as an affirmation of feminine difference. Nardal's is a question of ontology, of being. Woman simply *is* or *does*. Where such 'otherness' does not correspond to Nardal's ideas about women's equality, in effect, where she deems feminine characteristics as male-manufactured, she is quick to dispense with them.[33]

According to Sharpley-Whiting, from an ontological perspective rather than from a materialist feminist and existentialist perspective, Nardal associates the condition of women with women's own being and their actions. To Nardal, the identity of women based on oppression can assist women in becoming exemplary moral subjects. In ontologically associating being with action, Nardal conceives of freedom within the situation of women. This freedom allows women to decipher what is right and wrong for them. From this perspective, "women, like men, are wholly tied to social duty, the obligation to foster and nurture human progress."[34] In other words, from Nardal's perspective, even women in oppressed situations can derive a sense of freedom of choice simply because women's ontological freedom is greater and even more important than their political freedom. I would argue that while women have been able to survive with a limited amount of political freedom, without ontological freedom, the female population would be extinct or nonexistent.

As Sharpley-Whiting shows, given her Christian religious fervor and her endorsement of humanist principles,[35] Nardal conceives the social duty of women from a perspective that integrated Western values to her own concerns. She regards women's duties as different but not apart from those of men or from those of humanity in general. Framing her discourse on the rights of women in Martinique within dominant Western discourses, Nardal asserts that, in acting in accord with their respective parts (duties) in society, women came to be who they were as responsible agents, and that move benefited the whole of Martinique. Through her discourse on the rights of women in Martinique, Nardal shows how resisting the oppression of women involves the act of women melding with dominant discourses. To Nardal, women in Martinique had the right to draw upon humanist and liberal political discourses precisely because these women could contribute to these discourses.

To Nardal, the active participation of women in Western institutions can potentially free them from oppression. In her essay, "Woman in the City," in which she contemplates the ascension of Martinican women to the status of citizen, Nardal supports her concept of freedom:

> The social is the aspect of life that interests woman first and foremost. Regarding social duty, she is man's equal. As an individual, she is also intelligent and free. But as a social being, her services are bound to humankind. Like man, she must contribute to the progress of humanity. But this service, owing to the physical and psychological differences that exist between man and woman, will be of a different kind, though not necessarily of lesser value because of its difference. In fulfilling this social obligation, she remains true to her feminine vocation. What does this social duty entail? First, we must free ourselves from old prejudices, from lazy routines, in order to become familiar with social environments different from our own. The women of Martinique will therefore have to study problems concerning the family, the professions, the city. . . . It is to social education work that they are summoned.[36]

Despite differences between Nardal's and Beauvoir's conceptions of freedom, Nardal's biography reinforces one of Beauvoir's essential conditions for the possibility of freedom among women. Nardal's education and work reflects her apprenticeship of freedom, which shows her learned experience of acting responsibly, a condition that Beauvoir claimed facilitated the freedom of women.[37] Although it may have been a distinct characteristic of her personality, Nardal acquired her self-assertion—or "apprenticeship of freedom"—through her education, first at the Colonial College for Girls in Martinique, and later at the Sorbonne in France.[38] While Nardal's sense of self-assertion and freedom was developed in Western educational institutions, and was influenced by the women she met in French women's organizations, it was also developed through her studies of the concrete limitations placed upon people of color because of their race, and through her encounters with people of color, such as when she witnessed Anna Julia Cooper's dissertation defense at the Sorbonne in 1925.[39]

Her self-assertive actions on behalf of the advancement of women (both European and non-European) during her stay in France, England, and Martinique[40] placed Nardal in a position to act. Nardal's education reflects her philosophy, which resists the oppression of women through their active participation in Western institutions and the utilization of Western discourses. Her actions were not necessarily permissible for the average Martinican woman or, from Beauvoir's position, for the average French woman, as the average Martinican or French woman did not acquire the same type of education as Nardal. Nardal's education allowed her to act resourcefully and move beyond the racial and gender limitations of her situation as a woman of color; in other words, Nardal was a moral subject and Beauvoir would concede this claim.

To Beauvoir, at least in *The Second Sex* and *The Ethics of Ambiguity*, a person's situation cannot always be described in terms of freedom, precisely because of a person's existing social and physical constraints.[41] Although Beauvoir examines the limits of men's will to freedom through her analysis of the serious man, the sub-man, and the adventurer,[42] her analysis of the limits of a personal will to freedom is more detailed in her description of the relation of freedom, liberation, and independence to the situation of women.[43] To Beauvoir, women's oppression, which is determined by their feminine alterity, is what limits their will to freedom.

Although Beauvoir speaks of non-European women's will to freedom in brief and generalized terms,[44] precisely because her concept of freedom explicitly takes the situation of women not as the exception but rather the actual subject of freedom. Beauvoir's description of her moral concept of freedom places her analysis in a favorable position from which the concept of freedom developed within the writing of colonized women can be viably compared. So in the early 1960s when Beauvoir chose, to come to the assistance of Djamila Boupacha and to aid Gisele Halimi with the trial,[45] she believed that Boupacha was oppressed and had less freedom than Gisele Halimi and herself. While it can be argued that, to Beauvoir, Boupacha was oppressed, one may also posit that Beauvoir regarded Halimi as she may have regarded Nardal—as an exceptionally free minority woman. In Boupacha's trial, Halimi's actions as an astute lawyer showed that she possessed a sense of agency that enabled her to know what to do—from changing the location of the trial and rallying public opinion to writing a book on Djamila Boupacha's case.

To Beauvoir, there is no context in which the subject of freedom can be raised without including the context of moral freedom as it applies—or does not apply—to the situation of women. According to the analysis I present in this chapter—comparing Beauvoir's concept of freedom to Nardal's—despite the racial situational differences between their analyses, both women would agree that the possibility of political liberation is a pressing issue for both colonized and colonizer women.

Beauvoir asserts that the likeliness of independence, without the right kind of education and work directed toward freedom, was negligible for French women, a situation she relates to the lack of freedom of the African or harem slave of the eighteenth century.[46] Nardal, on the other hand, claims that the political liberation of women would begin when French-Martinican women embrace their social duties to become economically and politically free as citizens of Martinique. What is lacking in Beauvoir's analysis, but present in Nardal's, is an analysis of political liberation and moral freedom that takes into account the racial and gender oppression in the contemporary situation of non-European women. Precisely because of this, Beauvoir's analysis does not consider the role of White privilege in French women's political liberation. In Beauvoir's analysis of the political limitations behind the voting rights of French women in the 1940s, as stated in *The Second Sex*, she fails to address why it was that White French women were the first group of women in the empire to acquire the right to vote.

CONCLUSION

The Second Sex and *The Ethics of Ambiguity* present a parallel analysis between the gender oppression of White women and non-White women, enabling us to see how the oppression of the former, even when they were so-called independent, limits the freedom and agency of these two categories of women. The limitations that Beauvoir describes in the situation of White women (i.e., political, economic, and moral) refer to issues apparent in the oppressive situation of non-White women. By examining what Beauvoir writes in *The Second Sex* and *The Ethics of Ambiguity*, we can begin to imagine that very few French colonized female subjects were free, and that the context of freedom—of "true" freedom—could not be defined through the situation of oppressed women. Beauvoir's analysis of gender oppression does not, then, necessarily exclude the situation of colonized women. Here, a parallel can be drawn between the gender oppression of White women and the gender of oppression of non-White women in the French colonial empire, giving rise to an intersubjective ethics in Beauvoirian thought. Based on an analysis on the work of Beauvoir, we can see how all of these women were worthy of justice. Gender oppression, then, and the context of Beauvoir's ethics of freedom and existentialism, created political and historical relationships between White women and non-White women. From this angle, the ethics of Beauvoir can be compared to the ethics of Nardal—they both referenced the situation of disadvantaged women.

NOTES

1. Richard Burton, *French and West Indian: Martinique, Guadeloupe, and French Guiana Today* (Charlottesville, VA: University Press of Virginia, 1995), 132.
2. Robert Aldrich, *France's Overseas Frontier : Départements et Territoires d'outre-Mer* (New York, NY: Cambridge University Press, 1992), 188.
3. Burton, *French and West Indian*, 132.
4. Ibid. For example, Eugene Eboué (Socialist Party) was elected to the constituent Assembly of 1945, followed by Gerty Archimède (Communist Party), who was elected to the National Assembly from 1946–1951. On the other hand, the first Martinican woman elected to the regional council was Madeleine de Grandmaison and she was elected only in 1983.
5. Emily Kirkland and McTighe Musil, *La Marianne Noire* (Los Angeles, CA: University of California, Los Angeles, 2007), 200–2.
6. Burton, *French and West Indian*, 132.
7. Paulette Nardal, *Beyond Negritude: Essays from Woman in the City* (Albany, NY: SUNY Press, 2009), 6–7.
8. Nardal, *Beyond Negritude*, 11.
9. Ibid., 33.
10. Ibid., 21, 23.
11. Robert Bernasconi, *How to Read Sartre* (London: Granta, 2006), 54.
12. Margaret Simons, *Feminist Interpretations of Simone de Beauvoir* (University Park, PA: Pennsylvania State University Press, 1995), 82–83.
13. Bernasconi, *How to Read Sartre*, 54.
14. Ibid.
15. Simons, *Feminist Interpretations*, 82.
16. Beauvoir, *Second Sex*, 679–716. What I say here about the lack of freedom among women is shown in Beauvoir's analysis on the political and economic disenfranchisement of women in France, featured in the chapter, "The Independent Woman," of *The Second Sex*.

17. Beauvoir, *Ethics of Ambiguity*, 140.

18. Kristana Arp, *The Bonds of Freedom: Simone de Beauvoir's Existentialist Ethics* (Chicago, IL: Open Court; Distributed by Publishers Group West, 2001), 2.

19. Ibid.

20. Ibid.

21. Ibid., 2–3.

22. Kirkland and Musil, *La Marianne Noire*, 200.

23. Nardal, *Beyond Negritude*, 17.

24. Beauvoir, *Ethics of Ambiguity*, 37. To Beauvoir, the situation of the child reflects the "situation of women in many civilizations; they can only submit to the laws, the gods, the customs, and the truths created by the males."

25. Beauvoir, *Ethics of Ambiguity*, 37.

26. Arp, *Bonds of Freedom*, 115–16.

27. Beauvoir, *Ethics of Ambiguity*, 38.

28. Arp, *Bonds of Freedom*, 118.

29. Beauvoir, *Ethics of Ambiguity*, 37.

30. Arp, *Bonds of Freedom*, 117–18.

31. Nardal, *Beyond Negritude*, 21.

32. Arp, *Bonds of Freedom*, 118.

33. Nardal, *Beyond Negritude*, 18.

34. Ibid., 19.

35. Ibid., 18–19.

36. Ibid., 21.

37. Beauvoir, *Ethics of Ambiguity*, 37.

38. T. Denean Sharpley-Whiting, "Introduction: On Race, Rights, and Women," in *Beyond Negritude*, ed. Nardal (New York, NY: SUNY Press, 2009), 1.

39. Nardal, *Beyond Negritude*, 2.

40. Kirkland and Musil, *La Marianne Noire*, 200.

41. Beauvoir, *Ethics of Ambiguity*, 24–25, 37–39; Beauvoir, *Second Sex*, 679–80.

42. Beauvoir, *Ethics of Ambiguity*, 45–47, 57–61.

43. Beauvoir, *Second Sex*, 679–715.

44. Beauvoir, *Ethics of Ambiguity*, 37.

45. Djamila Boupacha is the Muslim Algerian young woman, who was accused by the French government, in 1960, during Algerian War, for attempting to plant a bomb in a cafe, in the French quarters in Algiers, Algeria. On February 10, 1960, Boupacha was arrested. Gisele Halimi, a French-Tunisian lawyer, contacted Beauvoir for assistance. Beauvoir responded and began to author articles on and publicly speak about, the problems with detaining Boupacha as a political prisoner. On April 21, 1962, prior to the end of the Algerian War, Boupacha was released from jail, all this with the public support of Beauvoir.

46. Beauvoir, *Ethics of Ambiguity*, 37–38.

Part III

DISCOURSE ON COLONIALISM, VIOLENCE, AND RACIAL IDENTITY—OPPRESSION AND WHITE PRIVILEGE

Chapter 4

Colonial Trends

On Violence

INTRODUCING BEAUVOIR ON VIOLENCE

This chapter traces the genealogy of Beauvoir's conception of colonial violence beginning with her publications on violence from the 1940s. In order to
situate Beauvoir's corpus of work on violence within French colonial philosophy, this chapter starts with a brief interaction between Beauvoir and Fanon.
As the chapter progresses, it traces on how the views of Beauvoir and Fanon
on violence separate. Fanon's conception of violence is mostly based on
French colonial conflicts and wars, whereas Beauvoir's analysis of violence
focuses on the context of post–World War II France, while including World
War II and the Algerian War of Independence. The move to connect but also
distinguish Beauvoir's views on violence from those of Fanon underscores
Beauvoir's importance on the female position within French postcolonial
philosophy. This chapter is written in the spirit of Ann V. Murphy's work on
the role of violence in Beauvoirian thought. What I add to Murphy's article
"Between Generosity and Violence" is that Beauvoir's corpus on violence
contributes both to discourses on violence in the French tradition, but also to
discourses on violence in French colonial philosophy.[1]

FANON ON VIOLENCE

When Simone de Beauvoir meets Fanon in the early 1960s, right before his
death, she observes that although his work is immersed in colonial violence,
he had an aversion to violence.[2] Of this issue, she specifically reports:

> Though an advocate of violence, he was horrified by it; when he described the
> mutilations inflicted on the Congolese by the Belgians or by the Portuguese

on the Angolans—lips pierced and padlocked, faces flattened by *palmatorio* blows—his expression would betray his anguish; but it did so no less when he talked about the "counter-violence" of the Negroes and the terrible reckonings implied by the Algerian revolution. He attributed this repugnance to his intellectual conditioning; everything he had written against the intellectual has been written against himself as well.[3]

Beauvoir's commentary reveals that although Fanon embraced the violence of the colonized during the process of decolonization, he did so with reservation and tribulation. He did not embrace the counter-violence of the Black Africans and revolutionary violence of the Algerians wholeheartedly. Beauvoir reports that Fanon's personal aversion to violence had to do with his intellectual background. As Beauvoir suggests, as an intellectual, Fanon anticipated the blowback of violence—or counter-violence—believing that it is never used or practiced without releasing negative social and political effects. So even when Fanon considered violence a decolonizing device, he was aware of its repercussions and boomerang effects.

Yet what Beauvoir reports here cannot make us believe, it seems to me, that as a doctor and intellectual participating in the Algerian War of Independence, and as a war veteran of World War II,[4] Fanon had cold feet. He was aware, as the analysis of Charif Quellel shows, that to be a revolutionary (i.e., to have the right to convey a message to those fighting for their liberation), one must participate in the revolution.[5] Quellel explains why Beauvoir reports that Fanon felt that she and Sartre, as left-wing intellectuals of the French empire, were not doing enough for the cause of Algerian liberation.[6] Although he did not suggest that they should become violent, Fanon, I argue, wanted both Sartre and Beauvoir to act, think, and write like colonial intellectual revolutionaries, believing that their writings ought to call the French to action against the institution of colonialism.

In *Force of Circumstance*, Beauvoir presents Fanon's complex relation to the use and purpose of violence in the process of decolonization and colonial resistance Beauvoir, unlike Hannah Arendt—even though Arendt saw the nuances in his concept of violence—did not fully condemn Fanon's advocacy of violence.[7] As Kathryn Gines argues, Arendt wrongly interprets Fanon's analysis of violence in *The Wretched of the Earth,* rejecting it because he argues for the use of violence by the oppressed to overcome the violent system of colonialism; as such, her critique of violence is unbalanced.[8] In a few words, Arendt accused Fanon of fetishizing violence as if it was a necessary step in the process of decolonialization. Arendt, in her critique of violence, seemed to disagree with what she thought was Fanon's view on violence. To Arendt, not only was Fanon fetishizing violence, he was also glorifying violence. Yet, I argue Arendt fails to see how violence, in the hands of the colonized, can serve as an instrumental good. In contrast, Beauvoir understood the complexity of Fanon's analysis of violence: that even in the face of colonial self-defense and even when it can be regarded as an instrumental good, violence is never the easiest choice. Fanon is not simply a glorifier of violence.[9] A closer reading of Fanon's conception of violence shows, as Nigel Gibson observes, that the goal is not violence for the sake of violence, but rather violence against violence.[10] Also, as Achille Mbembe maintains in *Critique of Black Reason,* there is a categorical difference between the violence of the colonizer and that of the colonized—the latter is simply responding to the violence of the former not initiating the physical first blow.[11]

Fanon's notorious chapter "On Violence" first appeared in *Les Temps Modernes* in May 1961 and was revised before being featured in *The Wretched of the Earth,* published in 1961.[12] In it, Fanon elaborates his position on the use of violence by the colonized during the decolonization process. The differences between the early and later versions appear in passages toward the end of the chapter "On Violence" in *The Wretched of the Earth,* which were edited and changed to include passages from Aimé Césaire's poetry on the prophetic significance of violence.[13] The version in *Les Temps Modernes* does not feature the work of Aimé Césaire but rather elaborates on the context of violence in Algeria.[14] Additionally, the section "On Violence in the International Context" is not included in *Les Temps Modernes*'s version.

In both versions, Fanon assesses violence within the context of decolonization. He has in mind the full decolonization from the European empire—that is, liberation and freedom for all colonized people. Additionally, he assesses violence within the context of the Manichean dialectic between the colonized and the colonizer,[15] demonstrating the multifaceted nature of the violence visited on the colonized—both material (physical) and psychological (mental).[16] To Fanon, decolonization is always a violent event,[17] simply because it is based on a power struggle, both between the colonized and the colonizer and among the colonized (i.e., within the mass population, the peasants, and the national bourgeoisie or the intellectuals).[18] Focusing on the decolonization process in Africa, but regarding Algeria as a model for the Third World,[19] Fanon observes the following about Algeria in particular: terror, counter-terror, violence, and counter-violence, a Manichean mechanism of colonialization and manifest, tenacious circle of hatred.[20] Explaining the violence and terror of the Algerian War of Independence, Fanon claims that the colonized and colonizer both terrorize one another as they participate in a dialectic of violence and counter-violence. That is, the colonized engage in self-defensive anti-racist and anti-colonialist violence in reaction to the White colonizer's racial colonial violence in order to counter the White colonizer's racial colonial violence.[21] All colonialist groups are racist, Fanon argues.[22] All colonizers impose themselves on their subjects, and it is this racially bound social, political, and economic imposition that the colonized seeks to subvert through violence.[23]

By claiming that decolonization is always a violent event, Fanon argues that decolonization is necessarily violent.[24] In doing so, Fanon complicates the condition of violence within the decolonization cause. Of course, the ultimate downfall of decolonization was to kill or be killed. However, understanding violence in this manner does not leave room for the alternative forms of violence committed during the decolonization process. Violence based on social, political, and psychological effects is also part of decolonization.

What made Fanon a forerunner in studies on colonialism is that he took note of not only the violent physical effects of colonialism/decolonization, but also its mental and nonphysical effects. In order to express the various violent phenomena in decolonization, Fanon focused on the fate of the colonized intellectual. To Fanon, the primary psychological violence that the colonized intellectual faced was having to adopt the ways of Europeans despite having been rejected by Europeans. Colonized intellectuals face even greater psychological problems because their ways make them suspicious to the indigenous population. The local colonized tend not to trust the ways of the colonized intellectual. Based on Fanon's analysis, the colonized intellectual is doubly alienated; one from his Europeans roots and second from his indigenous roots. The process of decolonization bares the tensions in the psyche of the colonized intellectual. The colonized intellectual wants colonialism to end, but it remains unclear to the indigenous population whether the colonized intellectual wants Europeans and their social, cultural, and political system entirely out of the colonies. It's not just that. The intellectual is also a symbol and reminder of the oppressor. It's also uncanny when the intellectual is also indigenous, since it's as if the oppressor and the oppressed were to cohabit the same body—you don't know if you should show sympathy or hostility to the indigenous intellectual. As such, the colonized intellectual is undecided about whether the indigenous population ought to use violence against the Europeans in order to expel Europeans out of the colonies.[25] As Donald K. Wehrs argues, Fanon's position on decolonization is that he blames the national bourgeoisie—intellectuals included—for having diverse interests that betrayed wartime solidarity between the national bourgeoisie and the mass indigenous population. In the face of violence against colonialism then, the colonized were at odds with each other, a reality that complicates Fanon's analysis of violence and reinforces the contradictions that Beauvoir observes in Fanon's discussions on the subject.

Also, emphasizing this reading of Fanon on violence shows the relationship between Fanon's and Beauvoir's conceptions of violence, respectively. In other words, given the contingency of freedom and the relevance of oppression among women and people at the margins, violence becomes a naturalized and inescapable act of freedom, something that Beauvoir saw worthy of noting in Fanon's conception of violence.

BEAUVOIR ON VIOLENCE

When "The Manifesto of the 121," also known as "The Declaration on the Right to Insubordination in the War in Algeria," was published in France on September 6, 1960, six years after the start of the Algerian War, Beauvoir was among the public signatories. She was not the only public female figure to sign—in fact, a good number of French women did so. Among them were the widely known writer Nathalie Sarraute and actress Simone Signoret.

The Manifesto had three main goals: (1) to speak out against the violence and torture committed by the French Army and government against the Algerians, (2) to publicly show the French Left support for the Algerian liberation cause, and (3) to stand up against the French colonial system in the interest of freeing the Algerians—of creating more freedom for the Algerians. Beauvoir, in signing the Manifesto, agreed with these main goals. Showing a sense of collective responsibility, Beauvoir positioned herself against the ethical and political impediment of the Algerians and against the violent racist oppression of the Algerians.

But there is a history, or "life passage," that led Beauvoir to sign this Manifesto. As Beauvoir defined herself in the late 1920s when she was preparing for her aggregation, she was not yet politically minded. World War II, the intellectual context of France after World War II, and Sartre's influence sparked her public interest in political subjects. In the 1940s, then, Beauvoir became political.[26] While there are many ways to explicate Beauvoir's political interests, I identify three main political matters as the focus of her political inquiry: (1) the question of violence as it relates to freedom in the face of political conflicts (i.e., the death sentence, torture, and war conflicts); (2) the question of freedom in the face of oppression (i.e., gender, sexual, racial, colonial, and imperial oppression); and (3) the question of French identity in the face of national political guilt and social crimes.

This section focuses on the evolution of Beauvoir's concept of violence as it relates to freedom. The question concerning Beauvoir's interest in the problem of being French in the face of national political guilt and social crimes will also be briefly touched upon. The goal then of this section is to understand her participation in the anti-colonial affairs carried out by the Left in France during the Algerian War, address how Beauvoir came to sign the Manifesto of the 121, and participate in the Djamila Boupacha case.

I separate Beauvoir's views on violence into two categories: (1) the earlier concept of violence published in "Pyrrhus and Cineas" (1944), "An Eye for an Eye" (1946), and *The Ethics of Ambiguity* (1947), which mostly focuses on the nature of violence and the role of violence in European society and (2) the later concept of violence as published in the article on Djamila Boupacha featured in *Le Monde* (1960), the preface to *Djamila Boupacha* (1962), and *Force of Circumstance* (1963), which mostly examines colonial violence and the corruptive nature of violence, thereby serving as Beauvoir's condemnation of violence. Her earlier and later conceptualizations of violence also affected her concept of freedom. I now turn, in chronological order of publication, to Beauvoir's essays.

To begin, in "Pyrrhus and Cineas," Beauvoir argues (in the section "Action") that "in one sense, violence is not an evil, since one can do nothing either for or against a man."[27] Beauvoir presents her view on the nature of violence by examining as a form of European folk tale, the life of Pyrrhus, an ancient Greek general who ignored the suggestion of his advisor, Cineas, not to go to war and therefore not to use violence against others. In "Pyrrhus and Cineas," Beauvoir examines Pyrrhus's freedom to use violence. By beginning her analysis of the nature of violence by claiming that violence is not an evil, Beauvoir wants to argue that violence is not a wrong in itself, which in turn means that violence may not necessarily be considered harmful against man. Beauvoir says that it's not necessarily an evil, but that doesn't mean violence doesn't affect others' freedom. From this perspective, then, Beauvoir's interest in the case of Pyrrhus and Cineas yields to an examination of the harmfulness of Pyrrhus's actions on the lives of others. If violence committed by one person cannot affect the freedom of another person, then why should violent actions be condemned?

Relating violence to a possible course of action, Beauvoir argues that we, as humans, cannot escape it. Indeed, we "are condemned to failure because we are condemned to violence. We are condemned to violence because man is divided and in conflict with himself, because men are separate and in conflict among themselves."[28] Claiming that violence is an inescapable condition of man, Beauvoir argues that we cannot do away with it. There is violence in our human condition because we are divided as men and in conflict with ourselves and with others. Moreover, in the abstract, since Beauvoir does not define violence as evil, she sees its nature as being a potential good, which in turn allows her to avoid condemning Pyrrhus's violent actions in battle. She also avoids denouncing violence in general. Because, to Beauvoir, it does not perfidiously harm men, killing becomes a warranted occurrence in humans' actions in the exercise of humans' freedom.

As Nancy Bauer observes, I undertake to do violence to others, as Pyrrhus wants to, "precisely in the name of liberty,"[29] or keeping up with the French Philosophy Tradition, in the name of "freedom," since in the French "liberty" and "freedom" are synonymous with one another. In "Pyrrhus and Cineas," as Sonia Kruks observes, Beauvoir concerns herself with the interconnection of "freedoms and the problem of violence."[30] In part, then, the goal of "Pyrrhus and Cineas" is to enable Beauvoir to question whether violence can ever be justified. As Debra Bergoffen claims, "The text addresses critical fundamental ethical and political issues: What are the criteria of ethical actions? How can I distinguish ethical from unethical political projects? What are the principles of ethical relationship? Can violence ever be justified?"[31] Understanding the actions of Pyrrhus as an ethical consideration, Beauvoir is able to question whether Pyrrhus's use of violence is ever justified. Since, to Beauvoir, violence is related to the fundamental nature of man's actions, in the process of living, we cannot escape acting and we cannot escape violence. Violence is part of the ethical subjectivity of man. The condition of being a subject signifies to a person that his or her action can be violent or that he or she can commit violence. In "Pyrrhus and Cineas," Beauvoir argues that violence is a normal course of action in the nature of man and is not evil. This chapter shows Beauvoir's first public interest on the question of violence.

In "An Eye for an Eye," as in "Pyrrhus and Cineas," Beauvoir signals a growing interest in the nature of violence. Here, Beauvoir examines the trial of Brasillach, a French author and journalist who supported the Fascist movement in France during World War II but was sentenced to death by the French administration after the war. Engaging with this case allows Beauvoir to continue to expand her views on the nature of violence and the role of violence in French society as it relates to human freedom. Examining the concept of violence through interconnected notions of "the guilty party," vengeance, and justice, Beauvoir marks the limits of the nature and role of violence in post-war France. Portraying vengeance as the act of harming someone in return for having first caused the harm that person has done to oneself or to another person, Beauvoir attempts to conceive of a way we can render justice to the injured parties without falling into the faith of vengeance, without reciprocating the violence of "the guilty party." In other words, in examining the relation among "the guilty party," vengeance, and justice, Beauvoir considers how we can punish the wrongdoer without hatred.[32] It seems like there are two things that need to be distinguished here: (1) avoiding punishing the wrongdoer with hatred; and (2) avoiding committing *another wrong* in our punishing of the wrongdoer, or punishing the wrongdoer without becoming wrongdoers ourselves in the process. More specifically, the chapter addresses why she refused to sign the petition to release Brasillach from his death sentence.[33] Beauvoir explains her decision:

> for the life of a man to have a meaning, he must be held responsible for evil as
> well as for good, and, by definition, evil is that which one refuses in the name
> of the good, with no compromise possible. It is for these reasons that I did not

sign the pardon petition for Robert Brasillach when I was asked to. I believe
that I understood during the course of his trial, at least roughly, how his political
attitudes were situated in the ensemble of his life. . . . The attitude of Brasillach
touched me in that he has courageously assumed his life. But precisely because
of that he recognized that he was one with his past. In claiming his freedom, he
also owned up to his punishment.[34]

While she claims that "all punishment is partially a failure"[35] because it
portrays a failed dialectic and a process of non-reciprocity among the "the
guilty party," the victims, and the public, Beauvoir feels that Brasillach,
in committing the crime—that is, in supporting Nazism, fascism, and anti-
Semitism—expressed his freedom, assumed his life, and "also owned up to
his punishment."[36] Understanding the actions that led to his death sentence
as a result of his freedom, Beauvoir argues that Brasillach opted for violence
against the Jews, which in turn affirmed his freedom and is consistent with
his punishment.

The case of Brasillach shows that Beauvoir understood the concept of
punishment in terms of the freedom of one's personal life choices and the
evil one may have committed. Not envisioning the punishment of Brasillach
as a form of vengeance against him, Beauvoir maintains that we can sentence a person to death in order to forgo the freedom of the person's "evil"
choices. In refusing to sign the petition for Brasillach's pardoning, Beauvoir
shows that she is not after his "flesh"—the termination of his life—but rather
for an affirmation of the freedom of choices. What this reflects about the
nature of violence according to Beauvoir is that violence is the manifesta-
tion of one's choices. Violence is in the hand of the person who committed
the crime.

In punishing Brasillach, we are only responding to the freedom of his
"evil" choices. We are not committing a crime against him. I note this in
Beauvoir's analysis of "the guilty party," vengeance, and justice, because
by acknowledging that we are not committing a crime in sentencing Brasillach to death, we also acknowledge a guilt-free conscience on the part of the
victims and the public. We acknowledge justice but not revenge. And while
in "Pyrrhus and Cineas," Beauvoir offers less context for the kinds of violent
actions Pyrrhus can commit, and in "An Eye for Eye" there is enough context
for the kinds of violent actions Brasillach has committed, there is a parallel
between Beauvoir's analysis on the nature of violence in both texts. The study
of violence does not change. The difference between these two essays is that
in "An Eye for an Eye," Beauvoir argues that committing violent actions
requires a sense of freedom, which is based on a sense of responsibility. In
other words, in committing violence, one must own up to the deed. The sense
of responsibility is necessary for determining either the goodness or the evil-
ness of a violent action.

While Beauvoir is not afraid to voice her opinion publicly on Brasillach's death sentence, she is cautious about her opinion on his trial. Despite favoring the punishment of Brasillach, Beauvoir's analysis suggests that Brasillach's death would not bring justice. To Beauvoir, "the affirmation of the reciprocity of inter-human relations is the metaphysical basis of the idea of justice."[37] But since justified violence tends to lead to un-reciprocity because it may not change the consciousness or the crime of "the guilty party" *and* not establish a dialogue between the "guilty party" and the sociopolitical code of justice, violence against Brasillach looks more like vengeance than justice. After the war, the French administration forbade the killing of collaborators by individual French people. Instead, the French administration delegated the punishment of collaborators to government's agencies in order for the French nation to punish without hate and therefore to punish without "crude" violence.[38] Punishing without hate, then, was the way the French administration saw fit to bring forth justice in France. This distinction is important because it shows how, after the brutality of World War II, the French administration attempted to foresee the possibility of sentencing or punishing the fascists, Nazis, and collaborators without perpetuating the violence of the Holocaust and World War II. Acknowledging, then, that even in the hands of the winners of the war, the use of violence can take an evil turn itself, the French administration forbade the punishment of fascists, Nazis, and collaborators by the general public. This position operates against Beauvoir's analysis on the nature of "justified" violence. To Beauvoir, violence is not an evil in itself—but to the French administration it is, and for this reason it should be regulated. For this reason, Beauvoir criticizes the French administration's attempt to try and sentence Brasillach to death. I see why it is an evil in itself for the French administration. They seem to condemn only "public violence" while totally being okay with state-sanctioned violence, for example, executions, thereby decreeing to public a distinction between illegitimate violence—violence commented by the people, and legitimate violence—violence of the State.

To Beauvoir, the government's position contradicts our natural inclination on the use of justified violence. Well enough, says Beauvoir, "it is necessary to punish without hate, we are told. Yet I think this is precisely the error of official justice. Death is a real, concrete event not the completion of a rite."[39] To Beauvoir, when we, for example, want to kill a criminal through a death sentence, we insist that "he himself must feel himself a victim, must endure violence."[40] But since, to Beauvoir, violence can only serve to make "the guilty party" recognize his real condition—that is, his condition as a Nazi or as a fascist in Brasillach's case—violence alone is not sufficient either. Following Beauvoir's line of inquiry, I believe, violence would not reciprocate the humanity between, for example, the collaborators and men of the resistance, between the anti-Semite and the Jew.

Not even justified violence can ever be an absolute constraint against "the guilty party."[41] Beauvoir suggests that in choosing to kill Brasillach through the death sentence, we are after his freedom and not his humanity; for, "to punish is to recognize man as free in evil as well as in good. It is to distinguish evil from good in the use that man makes of his freedom. It is to will the good."[42] Showing then the arbitrariness of the use of legitimate violence—since it cannot always render justice—Beauvoir is able to show that while violence may not be always truly justified, it functions as a mediator of our actions and freedom, between good actions that can go unpunished and evil actions that could be punishable.

In *The Ethics of Ambiguity*, published in the 1940s, Beauvoir looks at the role of violence in metropolitan Europe and (in passing) in colonial society or the periphery of Europe. In the essay based on a lecture, she looks at the situationality of violence and the contradictions of using violence as it affects politics and freedom. In line with her conception of violence in *Pyrrhus and Cineas* and "An Eye for an Eye," in *The Ethics of Ambiguity* Beauvoir begins her analysis by not condemning violence in itself but by she examining the situationality of violence. In the other essays, Beauvoir examines the manner and position of violence in relation to the environment of those who use violence or those violated by violence. Beauvoir's observation on the situationality of violence enables her claim that there is no *a priori* justification for violence.[43] The name and place of people who use violence or are affected by violence show that the reasons for the place of violence in society are not always predetermined. Not only does this mean that violence is contextual, but also that there is no predetermined end to violence. In Beauvoir's words, "We challenge every condemnation as well as every *a priori* justification of the violence practiced with a view to a valid end."[44] While violence cannot be condemned or done away with, there is also no way of predicting how an act of violence will turn out. Beauvoir condemns any dialectical view of violence, such as Marxism, which assumes that the use of violence in the dialectic of the revolution will lead to a positive outcome for the oppressed class.[45]

The particulars of violence arise in Beauvoir's analysis when she discusses in various passages of *The Ethics of Ambiguity* the use of violence and its effects on politics and freedom. According to Beauvoir, the use of violence on a national political scale amounts to blind violence.[46] Violence invades the freedom of an individual and leads to the destabilization of the mind,[47] in the sense that one cannot also integrate his/her actions with his/her identity after being violated or after committing a violent act. Similarly, as Georges Hourdin observes of the relation between violence and freedom in Beauvoir's essay, violence can be used only when it results in freedom greater than the one violence threatens.[48] Going back to "Pyrrhus and Cineas," the analysis on the relation between freedom and violence in *The Ethics of Ambiguity* further explains why Beauvoir does not condemn Pyrrhus's use of violence. Because we cannot know if his actions will lead to greater freedom than the ones he threatens, we cannot know if they will be justified. Building on her analysis on the nature of violence in "Pyrrhus and Cineas," and even in "An Eye for an Eye," in *The Ethics of Ambiguity,* Beauvoir specifies how the justification of violence ought to be determined. The ends of violence can never be judged in advance.

The ambiguities and contradictions of using violence arise in Beauvoir's analysis when she looks at violence in the British Empire:

> As we have also seen, the situation of the world is so complex that one cannot fight everywhere at the same time and for everyone. In order to win an urgent victory, one has to give up the idea, at least temporarily, of serving certain valid causes; one may even be brought to the point of fighting against them. Thus, during the course of the last war, no Anti-fascist could have wanted the revolts of the natives in the British Empire to be successful.[49]

One can fight one violent system, such as European fascism, while being, like the anti-fascist who supported British colonialism, for another violent system. Already critical of the violence of European colonialism in the 1940s, Beauvoir's anti-colonial position was to be strengthened during the Algerian War of Independence, when she closely looked at the evolution of and hypocrisy behind French colonialism.

In three main publications, Beauvoir examines the violence that arose in the context of the Algerian War; the preface to *Djamila Boupacha* (1962), the article on Djamila Boupacha published in *Le Monde* on June 3, 1960, and *Force of Circumstance* (1963). In these later works—unlike her essays on the nature of violence published in the 1940s—Beauvoir mostly focuses on colonial violence and the corruptive nature of violence, which then translate to her condemnation of violence. However, by focusing on the corruptive nature of violence, her ideas on violence in the 1960s are not far removed from her ideas in the 1940s on the relation between freedom of action and violence and on the justifications for the ends of violence. The difference is that the situational context of the Algerian War gives to Beauvoir an even cruder context out of which her concept of violence can be further developed.

In the introduction to *Force of Circumstance*, Toril Moi sums up Beauvoir's intellectual analysis on the greater context of French colonialism and on a lot of Algerians during the Algerian War in particular. Beauvoir's analysis is simple, says Moi, *"to massacre and torture another people in the name of racism and colonialism is absolutely evil. By consenting to such policies, the French in her eyes were no better than the Nazis. Even the few who opposed the war could not escape the collective burden of guilt.*"[50] Indeed, all of Beauvoir's essays or articles published in the 1960s—"Pour Djamila Boupacha" in *Le Monde,*[51] the preface to *Djamila Boupacha,*[52] and *Force of Circumstance*[53]—show Beauvoir's condemnation of colonial violence. Given Moi's analysis then, to Beauvoir: (1) colonialism was a violent and racist system; (2) any conflicts, war, and war crimes that derived from the system were unjust and eroded our sense of freedom; and (3) the French, whether for or against colonialism, were for most part culpable; they silenced themselves on the subject of colonialism and those who knew about the atrocities of the system were possibly in a worse position because they suffered from the burden of collective guilt. Beauvoir claimed that colonialism was a violent and racist system and because she held anti-colonialist and anti-racist views, Beauvoir condemned the violence of the colonial system. The violence of the colonial system mutated into racism, which reflected a very unjust social system. Since the violence of the colonial system does not always result in greater freedom than the ones it threatens, it unjustly usurps the freedom of people. Finally, the violence of the colonial system created both guilt and bad conscience in Europeans; those unaware of the atrocities of the colonial system suffered from a false consciousness and those who knew about the atrocities of the colonial system suffered from guilt.

Despite Beauvoir's claims in the 1940s that violence in itself is not an evil, the violence of colonialism was saturated with racism such that it could not be salvaged from evil. In Beauvoir's analysis, there could be no talk of the use of racist violence for the salvation of the colonized, for the freedom of the Algerians. Since the violence of the colonial system stands for justice, Beauvoir began to hold a position against French society. To Beauvoir, it was not enough to oppose the racism and violence of French colonial rule, the Frenchness of French colonial rule also had to be questioned. Why the "Frenchness" of colonial rule? From what I say below, it seems that Beauvoir questioned her own Frenchness. She seems to think that if one doesn't endorse the nation's policies, then one cannot properly identify with that nation. Why, for instance, can't Beauvoir see herself as French precisely because she's so invested in rectifying France's injustice? She's holding France to higher standards as a French person. How could one be against French racist and colonial violence and still remain French? Beauvoir then became "anti-French," as she claims her fellow compatriots labeled her.[54] By giving Beauvoir such a label, the French citizens in her society claimed that Beauvoir's anti-colonial and anti-racist positions reflected a bias on her part. How could one be French and not, for example, see the social and political progress that France brought to the society of the colonized? And why did Beauvoir have to assume that supporting the colonial system is racist? To Beauvoir, the answer was clear: the integrity of French citizenry could not remain intact, as it was for example at the start of the French Revolution, as long as there was colonialism in French society. To this end, Beauvoir's position on French colonialism was not different than Sartre's. As Jayati Ghosh explains, in the 1950s, she and Sartre were active in their support of the Algerian freedom struggle.[55] The Algerian War isolated progressive intellectuals who deplored the French colonial rule from other groups in French society.[56] This loss of a "common cause" with other French people (in contrast to the solidarity of the Resistance during World War II) forced intellectuals such as Sartre and Beauvoir to define their radical stance clearly and drove them to active political participation.[57]

The benefits then of being anti-French allowed Beauvoir to further defend her position to the French public. It led her to political activism. For example, being a person who expressed anti-racist and anti-colonialist sentiments is what led Beauvoir to sign "The Manifesto of the 121," and to participate in the release of Djamila Boupacha, a young Algerian woman who was arrested, "illegally" tortured, and sexually assaulted, and then sentenced to death because she was accused of planting a bomb in the university restaurant in Algiers in September 1959.[58] In 1960, Beauvoir supported a campaign to help Djamila Boupacha and lent her name to Gisele Halimi's book on the trial.[59]

CONCLUSION

I have shown that Beauvoir's position on violence in the 1960s built upon her writings on violence published in the 1940s, especially her establishment of the context through which violence could be condemned or rendered illegitimate and yet nevertheless be a naturalized course of expression within human suffering. Observing the news and events in France and the development of the Algerian war, Beauvoir argues that France's use of force and violence against the Algerians is unjust. But for her, as it was for Fanon, the counter-violence of native Algerians ought to be understood otherwise. Colonialism has forced the Algerians to express their freedom through violence. In sum, Beauvoir, like Fanon, argues that violence in the hands of the colonized and used with the goal of ending colonialism as a political and economic system makes violence more justifiable than in any other context. By explicating Beauvoir's analysis on violence, we can see how her work on violence places pressure on the reader in a similar manner to Fanon's conception of violence. Like Fanon, Beauvoir embraced the violence of the colonized against the European with extreme disquiet despite believing this type of violence to be justifiable or lawful. Furthermore, by comparing the violence of French against the violence of colonized, Beauvoir echoes Aimé

Césaire, who argued that, in the face of French colonialism, the Europeans and, in particular, the French, were the Nazis.[60] As Beauvoir sees it, echoing Fanon and even Césaire, the French colonialism gave both women and men a false consciousness.

NOTES

1. Ann V. Murphy, "Between Generosity and Violence: Toward a Revolutionary Politics in the Philosophy of Simone de Beauvoir," in *The Philosophy of Simone de Beauvoir: Critical Essays*, ed. Margaret A. Simons (Indianapolis, IN: Indiana University Press, 2006), 262.

2. Simone de Beauvoir, *Force of Circumstance, Vol. 2: Hard Times, 1952-1962* (New York, NY: Paragon House, 1992), 316.

3. Ibid.

4. David MaCey, "Frantz Fanon, or the Difficulty of Being Martinican," *History Workshop Journal*, 58 (October 1, 2004): 214–15.

5. Charif Quellel, "Franz Fanon and Colonized Man," *Africa Today* 17, no. 1 (January 1, 1970): 11.

6. Beauvoir, *Force of Circumstance*, 318.

7. David Macey, *Frantz Fanon: A Life* (London: Granta Books, 2000), 22; Hannah Arendt, *On Violence* (New York, NY: Harcourt, 1970), 14, 20.

8. Kathryn T. Gines, "Arendt Violence/Power Distinction and Sartre's Violence/Counter-Violence Distinction: The Phenomenology of Violence in Colonial and Post-Colonial Contexts," in *Phenomenologies of Violence* (Boston, MA: Brill, 2014), 124.

9. Nigel Gibson, *Frantz Fanon: The Postcolonial Imagination* (Malden, MA: Polity Press in association with Blackwell Publishing, 2003), 1.

10. Nigel Gibson, *Living Fanon: Global Perspectives*. Contemporary Black History (New York, NY: Palgrave Macmillan, 2011), 36.

11. Achille Mbembe, *Critique of Black Reason*, trans. Laurent Dubois (Durham, NC: Duke University Press Books, 2017), 165.

12. Macey, *Frantz Fanon*, 454.

13. Frantz Fanon, *The Wretched of the Earth Frantz Fanon*, trans. Richard Philcox, introduced by Jean-Paul Sartre and Homi K. Bhabha (New York, NY: Grove Press, 2004), 44–46.

14. Frantz Fanon, "De La Violence," *Les Temps Modernes* 16, no. 181 (May 1961): 1490–91.

15. Fanon, *Wretched of the Earth*, 1–62.

16. Halford H. Fairchild, "Frantz Fanon's The Wretched of the Earth in Contemporary Perspective," *Journal of Black Studies* 25, no. 2 (December 1, 1994): 192.

17. Fanon, *Wretched of the Earth*, 1.

18. Ibid., 23.

19. L. Adele Jinadu, "Fanon: The Revolutionary as Social Philosopher," *The Review of Politics* 34, no. 3 (July 1, 1972): 435.

20. Fanon, *Wretched of the Earth*, 47.

21. Reiland Rabaka, *Forms of Fanonism: Frantz Fanon's Critical Theory and the Dialectics of Decolonization* (Lanham, MD: Lexington Books, 2010), 132.

22. Irene L. Gendzier, "Frantz Fanon: In Search of Justice," *Middle East Journal* 20, no. 4 (October 1, 1966): 536.

23. Ibid.

24. Jinadu, "Fanon," 434.

25. Donald R. Wehrs, "Sartre's Legacy in Postcolonial Theory; Or, Who's Afraid of Non-Western Historiography and Cultural Studies?," *New Literary History* 34, no. 4 (October 1, 2003): 768.

26. Beauvoir, *Force of Circumstance*, 4.

27. Simone de Beauvoir, *Philosophical Writings* (Urbana, IL: University of Illinois Press, 2004), 138.

28. Ibid.

29. Nancy Bauer, *Simone de Beauvoir, Philosophy, and Feminism* (New York, NY: Columbia University Press, 2001), 153.

30. Sonia Kruks, "Beauvoir: The Weight of Situation," in *Simone de Beauvoir: A Critical Reader*, ed. Elizabeth Fallaize (New York, NY: Routledge, 1998), 47.

31. Debra Bergoffen, "Introduction," in *Philosophical Writings/Simone de Beauvoir* (Chicago, IL: University of Illinois Press, 2004), 80.

32. Beauvoir, *Philosophical Writings*, 249, 254.

33. Renee Winegarten, *Simone de Beauvoir: A Critical View*, Berg Women's Series (New York, NY: St. Martin's Press, 1988), 61.

34. Beauvoir, *Philosophical Writings*, 257.

35. Ibid., 258.

36. Ibid., 257.

37. Ibid., 249.

38. Ibid., 251.

39. Ibid., 254.

40. Ibid., 249.

41. Ibid.

42. Ibid., 259.

43. Simone de Beauvoir, *The Ethics of Ambiguity* (Secaucus, NJ: The Citadel Press, 1972), 147–48.

44. Beauvoir, *Ethics of Ambiguity*, 148.

45. Ibid., 147.

46. Ibid., 107.

47. Ibid., 110.

48. Georges Hourdin, *Simone de Beauvoir et La Liberté*, Tout Le Monde En Parle (Paris: Les Éditions du Cerf, 1962), 28.

49. Beauvoir, *Ethics of Ambiguity*, 98–99.

50. Toril Moi, "Introduction," in *Force of Circumstance* (New York, NY: Paragon House, 1992), v.

51. Simone de Beauvoir, "Pour Djamila Boupacha," *Le Monde*, 1960.

52. Simone de Beauvoir, *Djamila Boupacha* (New York, NY: Macmillan, 1962), 18–19.

53. Beauvoir, *Force of Circumstance*, 90–91.

54. Ibid., 90.

55. Jayati Ghosh, "Simone de Beauvoir: In Search of Freedom and Honesty," *Social Scientist* 14, no. 4 (April 1, 1986): 64.

56. Ghosh, "Simone de Beauvoir," 64.

57. Ibid., 64–65.

58. Beauvoir, "Pour Djamila Boupacha."

59. Karen Vintges, *Philosophy as Passion: The Thinking of Simone de Beauvoir* (Bloomington, IN: Indiana University Press, 1996), 134.

60. Aime Cesaire, *Discourse on Colonialism* (New York, NY: Monthly Review Press, 2000), 36–37.

Chapter 5

Beauvoir's Problem

White Guilt/Privilege, and Gender and Race Intersectionality

PREFACE

There are political relationships in history worth noting simply because they enable us to have some understanding of social and political occurrences within the development of contemporary society. One such relationship was between Simone de Beauvoir, Gisele Halimi, and Djamila Boupacha, whose dialogues illuminate gender and race relations among women of different social, economic, and political strata or origins. It is important to take note of these dialogues because currently we are still facing the problem of race and gender discriminations, and teasing out how some women in the past have navigated these issues can help some of us better (1) individually understand the race and gender conversations we have about ourselves and (2) the race and gender conversations we have about others.

The dialogue between Simone de Beauvoir and Gisele Halimi shows us—Whites and minorities alike—that the global, neo-colonial context tends to fracture rather than mend the lots of postcolonized subjects, such as Arabs, Asians, Latinas, mixed race people, and Blacks, for example. In the 1960s, the Russell Tribunal, also known as the International War Crimes Tribunal or Russell-Sartre Tribunal, organized by Bertrand Russell and hosted by Jean-Paul Sartre, was a dialogue among the world's intellectual elites on the status of American foreign policy during the Vietnam War. After apartheid in South Africa, the Truth and Reconciliation Commission held public dialogues between 1995 and 2002 to investigate human rights violations perpetrated under the Apartheid regime (1960 to 1994), including abductions, killings, and torture. While these dialogues had similar goals as the trial of Djamila Boupacha—to question the hold of racism and White supremacy on the world—Simone de Beauvoir, the main intellectual publicist of the Djamila

Boupacha trial, did not imagine that her writing about the trial and assertions about Boupacha to the French public could change the minds of racist
colonial France. All Beauvoir wanted was to free Boupacha from the death
penalty and send Boupacha back to Algeria and to the FLN; this, in itself, was
already a big achievement. So unlike Russell and Sartre, Beauvoir did not
believe she could easily affect perceptions of White hegemony. In addressing
the European public, Beauvoir was more pessimistic than Russell and Sartre
on racism, sexism, and class oppression. While she felt sure that the French
public would listen, she believed that members of the French public were
more passive than active listeners. It should be noted that Beauvoir was also
a representative at The Russell Tribunal; while she supported the goals of the
trial, Beauvoir was not always of the same mind-set as Russell and Sartre on
the subjects of the trial. More specifically, Beauvoir's intellectual experience
with gender and sexual oppression prevented her from viewing the racial and
systematic political oppressive topics of the trial in the same manner as Russell and Sartre.

In what follows, I recount the relationship between these three women in
order to show how women of different social, economic, and political strata
collaborated with one another to fight an injustice based on imperialism and/
or colonialism, which was an injustice fundamentally based on the intersection of gender and of racism, or the belief in White superiority. Whenever
Beauvoir addressed the French public, she was guided by the relationships
that she had with both Gisele Halimi and Djamila Boupacha such that the
communications among these women influenced the message about the trial
that Beauvoir was sending to the French public.

INTRODUCTION

When Simone de Beauvoir was invited by Gisele Halimi to participate in
the trial of Djamila Boupacha, a young Arab-Algerian woman sentenced to
death by the French administration after being accused of planting a bomb in
the European quarters in Algeria during the last stages of the Algerian War,
she did not hesitate to accept. With Halimi's legal skills and Beauvoir's testimony, Boupacha's death sentence was overturned.[1]

The trial lasted two years—1960 to 1962. However, after Boupacha's
release, Beauvoir considered meeting Boupacha in person unnecessary.
Halimi, a French-Tunisian lawyer of Jewish and Arab origin, insisted that
Beauvoir meet Boupacha. But Beauvoir turned down the offer. What I present here is taken from Halimi's autobiography, *Milk for the Orange Tree*[2]
and is, therefore, largely influenced by Halimi's perspective. However,
I will attempt to balance this position by drawing upon texts written by

Beauvoir. In what follows, I examine the relations among Halimi, Beauvoir, and Boupacha in order to make sense of why Beauvoir collaborated with Halimi in order to overturn Boupacha's sentence and yet, after the trial, refused to meet her. I also look at what message Beauvoir was sending to the French public during the post-trial period and her actions with both Halimi and Boupacha.

Beauvoir was not necessarily misguided in refusing to meet Boupacha. Her decision was a matter of personality traits and sociopolitical and personal circumstance. As Halimi records in her autobiography, ultimately to Beauvoir, the fate of Boupacha ought to have been primarily decided by the National Liberation Front (FLN), given the political circumstances after the end of the trial—the end of the Algerian War.[3] Halimi hoped that Beauvoir would meet Boupacha to have an influence on the choices of Boupacha as a woman. But meeting Boupacha in order to affect her future was not something Beauvoir believed she could do. After Boupacha was free, Beauvoir believed Boupacha should only give an account of herself to her community—the FLN.

To address the difference of opinions between Halimi and Beauvoir, I divide this chapter into five sections. The first section addresses the perceptions of Beauvoir, Halimi, and Boupacha by the French public, which I claim was influenced not by gender but by their racial, ethnic, and national differences. The second section situates Beauvoir and Halimi in French colonial intellectual history. The third section presents the difference of opinions between Halimi and Beauvoir on Boupacha's situation after she is free from prison. The fourth section considers Beauvoir's relation to the Algerian War and to Boupacha in particular. The fifth examines Halimi's personal perspective of Boupacha's situation after she is free from prison. I conclude that both Halimi and Beauvoir agreed to disagree on what Boupacha should do after she was free and the Algerian War ended.

BEAUVOIR'S PUBLIC POLITICAL PERCEPTION: RACE, ETHNICITY, AND NATIONALITY

To present a deeper understanding of Beauvoir's choice, I highlight the tension in the way Beauvoir primarily identifies Boupacha. Beauvoir saw Boupacha as a member of a colonized Arab group, rather than as an oppressed woman. Beauvoir did not even see how Boupacha's gender and race intersected in her situation. Rather than seeing that the gender and racial situation were simultaneously affecting, for example, the treatment of Boupacha in prison, Beauvoir believed that she was tortured and raped in prison primarily because she was Arab. Arab men were also being tortured and sometimes sexually abused in prison, and Beauvoir knew this. So, Beauvoir did not see the difference between the treatment of Boupacha as a woman and the treatment of Arab men in French cells.

Rather than examining Boupacha's situation as unique to her life as a minority or as an Arab woman, Beauvoir equated it to the situation of Arab men, thereby emphasizing the race problem over the gender issues. Yet, Boupacha was a racialized and gendered subject; as such, she experienced racism and sexism simultaneously. As a feminist, how could Beauvoir leave gender out of the picture and identify Boupacha as an *Arab* rather than as an *Arab woman?*

Beauvoir's move to see Boupacha more as an Arab person was not necessarily a naïve choice. The context of the Algerian War convinced Beauvoir to see Boupacha in terms of her race and ethnicity first. Had she considered Boupacha's gender first, she might have reached out to Boupacha not as a white French woman colonizer, but as one woman reaching out to another woman in need. But since the context of race, ethnicity, and/or nationality is always present in the political encounter of two people from different origins, there is no way that Boupacha, as an Arab, and Beauvoir, as a White person, could meet as racial and ethnic equals. Despite her good deed, Beauvoir couldn't help but act as a White French woman, and meeting Boupacha would only have highlighted the national, racial, and ethnic conflicts and differences between these two women.

Why Beauvoir did not feel these same misgivings about Halimi, a Jewish Arab professional is an issue I address by arguing that the social, political, and economic/class similarities between the two women—Beauvoir and Halimi—alleviated the problems of national, ethnic, and racial identity. Through their similarities these two women were able to reach a common goal, opting to relate to one another in terms of their gender, not as oppressed but as empowered women, which created a sense of solidarity and gave both of them the courage to risk their lives during the Algerian War to help free a "racially" oppressed person—Boupacha.

Among Beauvoir, Halimi, and Boupacha then, a gender focus gave them more power, while their race, nationality, and ethnicity undermined their cause. Beauvoir was White, and to support the cause of the Algerians was seen as suspicious by the French government; her position contradicted the views of the French public. Halimi was Jewish and Arab, so while her support of the Algerians may have been considered obvious, because she was French, the French government put her under police supervision. Boupacha was Arab and working for the FLN, which is why she was arrested.

Because the French colonial ethos emphasized the race, nationality, and ethnicity of these women, they could not collaborate simply in terms of their status as women. It was their nationality, ethnicity, and race that created the power dynamic among them. Beauvoir was well placed in France because of her status as a White person. Halimi was Arab and Jewish but educated and exceptionally privileged. Following Sartre's thesis in *Anti-Semite and Jew*, Halimi could pass as French but always not quite. So Halimi had less power and credibility than Beauvoir in the eyes of the French public, which is why she sought her assistance. Boupacha was oppressed and in prison simply because she was Arab. The ways I racially define these three women here is how I argue these women primarily related to one another and were viewed by the French public, which influenced the public's representation and assessment of the trial.

THE LEADING WOMEN

In the recorded history of the Western World, women have been known to collaborate with one another for, according to my observation, three main causes: (1) helping themselves—coming together to educate themselves and improve their own situations in, for example, book clubs and small women's organizations; (2) serving the greater good of society—coming together and working in factories in order to make up for the lack of "man" power as in the United States during World War II; and (3) helping others in greater social needs than themselves—such as in the 1791 sugar boycott, when abolitionist women of Britain participated in the boycott of sugar and rum in order to destabilize the economic system based on the revenue of plantations and slaves' private property ownership. These British abolitionists came together to end slavery and free male and female slaves.

Beauvoir and Halimi were collaborating for two main causes: (1) supporting the abolition of a great social injustice—colonialism; and (2) helping a woman in greater need than them. In participating in the public hearing of the Boupacha trial, both Beauvoir and Halimi took their place in history by acting as members of a women's coalition.

I focus on the achievements of Beauvoir and Halimi because they can offer an alternative perspective, different than the dominant discourses of such social and political movements, which, for the most part, features leading men. But when we focus on leading women in history, we can see how women were both victims and perpetrators within these social and political movements. In this book, rather than being primarily concerned with Sartre, Fanon, Aimé Césaire, Albert Memmi, and Camus, the focus is on Beauvoir and Halimi. These women, like these famous men, are important because they participated in the anti-colonial movements in both colonial and metropolitan France. Contemplating their story shows how people whose living situations were based on the connection between race and gender conflicts contributed to the French anti-colonial movements of the 1950s and early 1960s, led by French intellectuals.

Prior to her involvement in the trial of Boupacha, Halimi participated in the independence movements taking place in the Maghreb. She participated in the movement for the independence of Tunisia and became involved in the Algerian Independence struggles. By the time she sought the assistance of Beauvoir, Halimi was a young attorney known for her activism,[4] which means she could have had similar intellectual status as Beauvoir. But Halimi was not White. Nevertheless, the public status of these women eased the initial contact between the two.

Beauvoir, as an intellectual, was already familiar with the atrocities of the Algerian War. But what Halimi provided Beauvoir was a concrete way to help the cause for Algerian liberation. Halimi proposed to Beauvoir that she could participate in the liberation of the Algerians by beginning to help just one Algerian—Djamila Boupacha, which seemed feasible to Beauvoir.

Halimi was interested in Beauvoir's public status—Beauvoir as not only a self-described feminist and existentialist, but also a public intellectual with a national reputation. Halimi wanted the trial of Boupacha to gain some publicity. Since Beauvoir opted to participate in the public representation of the trial in France, she clearly took participation to be her job. And so they started to work together in order to secure the release of Boupacha from the grip of the French government. Beauvoir wrote an article published in *Le Monde* in June 1960.[5] Beauvoir headed the Committee for Djamila Boupacha.[6] Halimi wrote an article published in *Les Temps Modernes*.[7] Both women collaborated to write a book on Boupacha, which was published in 1962.[8]

THE CONFLICT BETWEEN BEAUVOIR AND HALIMI

The trouble is not that Beauvoir collaborated as a White woman colonizer with a Jewish and Arab woman in order to free an Arab woman, or that both Halimi and Beauvoir saw eye to eye on how the case should be presented to the French public in both colonial and metropolitan France. The conflict that arose between these women was about their intra-gender relations: what Beauvoir and Boupacha could do as women for Boupacha after she was freed. Specifically, to Beauvoir and Halimi, solving the trial of Boupacha was about navigating race relation. But the aftermath of the trial was about navigating gender relations. To Halimi, Boupacha ought to be given the choice to do what she wanted with her life; this, to Halimi was the only way Boupacha could show political progress in her situation after the trial. To Beauvoir, the FLN had to choose this for Boupacha. Beauvoir felt that given the political circumstances between France and Algeria, the implicit contract between Boupacha and the FLN could not easily be breached.

Beauvoir believed this perhaps because she thought that Boupacha should always be in solidarity with the FLN. After all, one could argue that it was because Boupacha was a member of the FLN that she was able to gain the attention of the French and Algerian public. Beauvoir's siding with the FLN to decide upon Boupacha's future created a conflict between Halimi and Beauvoir. Beauvoir believed that Boupacha was safer with the FLN. But to Halimi that did not leave much choice to Boupacha.

Passages from Halimi's autobiography describe her difference of opinion from Beauvoir:

21 April 1962, Djamila Boupacha was released from prison.

Meanwhile, Simone de Beauvoir, who has not met her, rings again. We arrange for the three of us to meet for lunch two days later. Djamila picks up the phone and shyly says a few words of thanks. She hangs up, vaguely disappointed. To the warm, sensitive heroine, the neutral tone of certain intellectuals seems an indication of coldness.

The CIMADE (*Comité Intermouvement Auprès des Évacués* [Joint movement for assisting evacuees]), a Protestant organization which had often expressed sympathy for the Algerian cause, would like to see Djamila. At their headquarters in Paris. Just for half an hour; then, we are assured, she will come back with us.

We take her there, Small dark offices opening off an entrance hall. A waiting room. Djamila is shown into one of the offices by a member of the staff.

We did not see her again.

Kidnapped, kept by the "brothers" of the Federation under lock and key in a council flat in the Paris suburbs. Then put on a plane, well-guarded. Destination: Algiers.

For the FLN, mission accomplished.

The same evening, I ring up the Beaver[9] and describe the trial of strength and Djamila's kidnapping. She neither condemns nor expresses indignation. She already knew. The FLN was within its rights. "You have been unwise, Gisèle," she said. I had no right, we French had no right, to intervene on behalf of an independent Algerian woman.

I try to explain Djamila's plans. What's more, we don't just bow to reasons of state, we're in the habit of talking them over, be they by the FLN's or our own. When we don't reject them outright, on principle.

"We'll have lunch tomorrow as arranged." The Beaver terminates the discussion.

Which we never resumed.

A few days later, a communiqué is circulated in Tunis, sent by the French Federation of the FLN, denouncing "*the publicity operation attempted for her own personal ends by the lawyer Gisèle Halimi, in connection with our sister Djamila Boupacha*" (*Le Monde*, 3 May 1962).

I did not reply.

This infant revolution was already burdened with the perverted tendencies of all the others. Aided and abetted by intellectuals with clean hands and 'white' complexes.

Simone de Beauvoir presided over the fight for Djamila. She never met her.

For her, was not understanding the nature of the battle more important than the person at stake?

"You never even had a chance of embracing her," I told her.

"It's not important," she replied in surprise.[10]

Halimi records that Beauvoir advised her to stay out of the relation between Boupacha and the FLN. But Halimi suggests that Beauvoir get over her White guilt complex, which she compared to the guilt of other White intellectuals in the Algerian revolution and past revolutions. Halimi saw that Beauvoir tried to assess her guilt objectively by not taking chances with either Boupacha or the FLN. But to Halimi, Beauvoir was being too careful, because, as a White person, she refused to see the difference between the fate of Boupacha and the racial-colonial lots of members of the FLN. Boupacha and Beauvoir talked by phone. But given what Halimi and Beauvoir had gone through to free Boupacha, a simple phone conversation between the two was not enough for Halimi.

Rather than following Halimi and claiming that Beauvoir suffered from a White guilt complex, which Shannon Sullivan would support,[11] Beauvoir was realistic enough to admit that the trial and its aftermath with the involvement of the FLN was never beyond the White problem—beyond the problem of White supremacy. In her article on Boupacha published in *Le Monde*, Beauvoir attacks the French and their government for being accomplices in the torture and murder of colonized Algerians, Beauvoir did not believe that her anti-French position did not make her inculpable.

WHITE PRIVILEGE AND BEAUVOIR'S
SIDE OF THE STORY

Beauvoir's anti-French position came with its own set of personal problems. In *Force of Circumstance*, Beauvoir admits that she suffered from a guilt complex. Her guilt complex allowed her to admit her social position as a privileged White woman who could have lived in France without her having to write or testify to the miseries of the colonized Algerians. Yet Beauvoir was able to address her guilt complex, assuming the problems of France with the Algerians as her own.

Beauvoir addressed her guilt, as she reports in her autobiography, *Force of Circumstance*, by transforming it into personal and political testimony. Not only did she blame the French, as Julien Murphy reports, but Beauvoir also did not spare herself of these accusations.[12] She "felt an overwhelming responsibility about the war."[13]

Following Sartre's train of thought, as featured in the article "Colonialism is a System," Beauvoir supports the position that the French colonial system had made "colons" out of *all* French citizens and that the French could not be divided between "good" and "wicked."[14] In other words, if the French colonial system was still in place, the colonial lifestyle of all White French citizens—enjoying wine made from grapes grown in Algeria, voting against the end of colonialism, rationalizing racism and the violence of the French government and military, or turning a blind eye to the oppression of the Algerians—made all French people culpable, and even knowing this did not even make them inculpable. Beauvoir, like Sartre, approved of this anti-colonial philosophy.

The sense of responsibility that she felt for both the French and the Algerians enabled Beauvoir to address her guilt complex. Contrary to what Shannon Sullivan argues on the ways White guilt—guilt experienced by White people for discovering their position in the power structure of racial oppression—tends to direct White people to their feelings in a non-productive way,[15] Beauvoir was able to take a stand. Among the French then, she became an exception.

In spite of Halimi's accusation that Beauvoir suffered from a White complex, Beauvoir's reaction to Boupacha was politically motivated rather than based on a lapse of emotional judgment—based on the emotions or turmoil surrounding White guilt. The attempt to explicate or evince whether a mature and complex woman like Beauvoir suffered from White guilt can politically undermine the sophisticated approach with which Beauvoir related to the positions of Halimi, Boupacha, the FLN, the French public, and French intellectuals during and after the trial of Boupacha. Even for those who would support Halimi's position that Beauvoir acted out of White guilt when she was responding to the French government's offense toward Boupacha, at the very least, Beauvoir's guilt drove her to political and ethical action. In other words, Beauvoir acted from an *active* guilt complex rather than a *passive* guilt complex.

In *Simone de Beauvoir and the Politics of Ambiguity*, Kruks comments on Shannon Sullivan's work on White privilege in "Whiteness as Wise Provincialism: Royce and the Rehabilitation of a Racial Category." As Sonia Kruks understands Sullivan's position, there is an interconnection between White guilt and White privilege in Sullivan's analysis of guilt. Such an interconnection, between White guilt and White privilege, when utilized properly, can lead to self-transformation—and, specifically, to self-innovation.[16] So, in the face of French racism and violence, Beauvoir had to invent herself as "Anti-French" in order to conquer her guilt and embrace the positive possibilities of White privilege—that is, taking racial identity away from a racially neutral identity, fighting White supremacy and colonialism despite her personal pessimism and doubts. This put her in a position from which she could consistently voice her position against the French, their violence, racism, and political system. Re-inventing herself as anti-French led Beauvoir to transform herself anew in the face of colonial violence and racism. By acknowledging her White privilege, Beauvoir reflected on the fact that she had a racial identity, which put her at odds with the common narrative of Whites who assume they are race-neutral or raceless.

As Ursula Tidd explains in her article "The Self-Other Relation in Beauvoir's Ethics and Autobiography":

> [A] sustained example of the construction of autobiographical space for the Other is Beauvoir's account of the Algerian War in *Force of Circumstance*, in which she attempts to transcend her "situation" as a bourgeois Frenchwoman and seeks to represent the Algerian perspective. While she can never have the experience of being a colonized Algerian subject to French rule, she provides a historical account that creates space for the experience of the Other, for example, Djamila Boupacha.[17]

Beauvoir did not just empathize with the oppressed situation of the colonized, she also created a space for them in public intellectual discourse. Beginning her inquiry on Algeria in the first person, she was able to transcend her individual position to appeal to the politics and morals of the French and to appeal for the freedom of the Algerians. In other words, she attempted to make the French accept the freedom of the colonized as a right by directing the French to her publications (and the publications of others) on the social and political situation of the colonized Algerians.

Further, as Toril Moi observes in her article, "Meaning What We Say," Beauvoir says "to write is to appeal to the freedom of the other. [. . .] [But] to appeal to the freedom of others is to risk their rebuff."[18] In speaking up for the Algerians, in speaking up for Djamila Boupacha, in particular, Beauvoir was not looking for the "handshake" from the colonized French subjects. So much more had to be socially and politically done for the two women to meet each other face to face; colonialism and White supremacy had to end and women in both France and Algeria had to be freed from gender and sexual oppression. Perhaps working against narratives of the politics of reconciliation, Beauvoir did not believe that she could meet Boupacha on amicable terms. The political time, the early 1960s, which marked the end of the French decolonization period, was just not right. Quoting Mahmood Mandani, Beauvoir did not want *reconciliation without justice*. According to her philosophy, then, she did what a self-defined anti-colonialist and anti-racist public intellectual could do. Her actions toward Boupacha represented the duty of the Left intellectual, and not a misguided or undermining choice.

Accordingly, no matter what we think of Beauvoir's actions during the Algerian War, what she did for the Algerians in general—signing petitions, like *The Manifesto of the 121* for the cessation of the Algerian War and for Djamila Boupacha, in particular, even when she had the support of intellectuals who contributed in *Les Temps Modernes*, such as Sartre, Gisele Halimi, and Francis Jeanson, should be regarded as an exception to the rule. Not all French Leftist intellectuals, such as Albert Camus, embraced the end of colonialism and supported the cause of the Algerians.

Overall, in admitting her White privilege during and after Boupacha's trial, Beauvoir acted, for the most part, from a position not necessarily based on a guilt complex. In other words, she did not feel de-habilitated by her White privilege—she knew when to use it and when to step back. Her actions show that she admitted her White privilege but always attempted not to be affected by the perils of her guilt complex—an existential situation experienced among White people which leads some of them to a state of nonpolitical action and of racial-neutrality. And for the greater purpose of participating in conversations on White privilege and White guilt, Beauvoir was able to show through the personal and political affirmation of one's own White privilege that *some*, like herself, can come to terms with their racial guilt. As Homi Bhabha argues, the power of Beauvoir's thinking and feeling lies in her ability to articulate—with a certain ambiguity—the anxiety of the psychic landscape with the agency of the political terrain.[19]

I align with Bhabha, who turns to Beauvoir's midlife crisis—as recounted in *Hard Times*—considering the fragile and fractious beauty with which she comes to terms with the contingent forces of human circumstance.[20] Intimations of aging and illness, the public shame of the Algerian War suffered as a personal tragedy, insomniac nights laced with beladenal, the deep fear of outliving Sartre—all these affective and political forms of "negativity" become part of the paradoxical project of human freedom, the ambiguity of emancipation.[21]

PERSONAL FREEDOM AND HALIMI'S
SIDE OF THE STORY

Perhaps the differences between Halimi and Beauvoir on the fate of Boupacha after the trial have to do with the fact that Halimi met Boupacha and listened to Boupacha's personal story. After Boupacha was released from jail, she stayed for a short time at Halimi's house. Halimi records in her autobiography that they spent time talking about Boupacha's future. Boupacha did not want to return to Algeria. In her own words: "I don't want to return to Algeria now. [. . .] [T]he 'brothers' will make me take up the life of a woman back there."[22] Whatever actions Boupacha was performing for the FLN, they were different than women in Algeria. If she returned to Algeria now, her Algerian "brothers" would make her assume the role of a regular woman, which only confirmed that she would have little freedom in Algeria. The so-called regular women in Algeria, had to have a limited amount of education, care for family, get married in order to care for her husband and children and do primarily housework. Halimi was not satisfied with Boupacha's answer and protested: "You're exaggerating. You and the other Algerian women have proven yourselves."[23] In other words, after all that Algerian women had done and sacrificed for the revolution, there was no way that some mujahidin, like Boupacha, would be asked to go back to Algeria to perform traditional or regular female activities. Boupacha elaborated, "I shall have no responsibilities. No woman will be a member of the government, you'll see. Not a single one will share power with the 'brothers.' In any case, I must go on studying, I have much to learn."[24] Presenting an insider's perspective of the differences between the future of Algerian men and women in postcolonial Algeria, Boupacha admitted she would not enjoy the same freedom as her "brothers." Although her efforts were not pointless during the Algerian War, they would not necessarily impact her personal freedom. Politically, she would be free from the grip of French colonialism but not from the grasp of her Algerian "brothers."

After Boupacha was free from prison and the Algerian War was coming to an end, she knew that her role as a guerrilla fighter among her "brothers" was also abruptly ending. It was the fate of many Algerian women to participate in the leadership of postcolonial reconstruction of Algeria. After several phone calls from Algerian male representatives of the FLN in Paris—requesting that Boupacha either participate in the movement in Paris or return to Algeria[25]— Halimi began to see, with some regret, that the fate of Boupacha was not in her hands. As a woman then, Halimi couldn't do any more for Boupacha.

CONCLUSION

While Halimi was concerned about Boupacha's personal freedom and her status as an oppressed woman in both France and Algeria, Beauvoir only considered her ethnic, racial, and colonial fate. The racial and colonial aspects of the trial gave Beauvoir the chance to challenge only the White world but not the Arab world or, more specifically, the Arab Algerian community. In other words, Beauvoir could try to free Boupacha from the subjugations of the White world but not the subjugations of the Arab world. I concur with

Bonnie Mann's assertions on Beauvoir's intellectual commitment; Mann explains, "Beauvoir's commitment to engaged philosophy, her insistence on a phenomenological examination of both lived experience and the 'total concrete situation' in which it takes shape, her refusal to retreat, as a feminist, from the political realities of French colonial commitments, her insistence on standing up to her government and her fellow citizens in a time of war, her commitment to an [existential] ethics of gender, evidence a kind of feminist thinking that is exemplary."[26]

Beauvoir and Halimi reconciled their positions on what Boupacha ought to do after the trial, Beauvoir and Halimi agreed to disagree. Beauvoir stuck to her position and Halimi felt coerced into letting Boupacha go back to Algeria. This disagreement, I believe, may have caused some differences in their relationship but Beauvoir and Halimi continued to collaborate well past the trial and on into the French feminist abortion movements of the 1970s.

Of course, Beauvoir's feminist philosophy could have led her to conclude that the intra-racial and gender treatment of Boupacha by her "brothers" was wrong. But to Beauvoir, it was not her place—or even Halimi's—to attempt to change these circumstances. Beauvoir's commitment to existential ethics meant that every woman, including Boupacha, had to come to terms with her own gender struggles in order to better engage with her individual identity. Beauvoir made Boupacha responsible for her situation. In gaining her freedom from French colonialism, Boupacha could be regarded, I suggest in existential terms, as both the victim and the perpetrator of the intersection between her gender and racial situation.

The aim of this analysis of Beauvoir's journey through French colonialism and philosophy is to point to how personal agency can be mitigated in cross-cultural political interventions. I want to show that through her philosophy, Beauvoir made Boupacha responsible for her situation. In gaining her freedom from French colonialism, Boupacha could be regarded, in existential terms, as both the victim and the perpetrator of the intersection between her gender and racial situation. Beauvoir worked against the common Western tradition, as Lila Abu-Lughod observes in her article "Do Muslim Women Really Need Saving?"[27] which supports the position that Arab women like Boupacha need to be saved from Arab men and the perils of Arab societies.

Borrowing from Abu-Lughod's analysis, I want to show how Beauvoir was able to challenge the narrative of victimhood particularly associated with a lot of Muslim women. I present an analysis that relates the work of Beauvoir on colonialism to present political interventions of White women aiding non-White women. Particularly, I look at former first lady Laura Bush urging Americans to go to war in order to come to the assistance of Afghan women. Although most feminists condemn Laura Bush's response,[28] I focus on the claims of Abu-Lughod in order to exemplify the sentiments of feminists against Laura Bush. According to Abu-Lughod's records, Laura Bush gave a radio address on November 17, 2001, with the message that the fight against terrorism is also a fight for the rights and dignity of women—women of Afghanistan in this case.[29] During this "War of Terror," Laura Bush argued that "the brutal oppression of women [of Afghanistan] is a central goal of the terrorists."[30] I end my analysis in this chapter by arguing that cross-cultural political relations between White women and minority women ought not to be outright negated. In other words, I am questioning why Laura Bush chose to talk about this issue as opposed to another, such as boys' lack of access to schools and medical facilities and Afghan men being coerced to join the Taliban. If need be, White women ought to lead political interventions that would ultimately help minority women to own up to individual or communal accounts of minority women's living experiences in the first person. Minority women have their own sense of agency and subjectivity, as portrayed by the actions of Gisele Halimi and Djamila Boupacha, that stems from their personal journeys as women; if they are content, comfortable, or even dissatisfied with their situations, it is not up to White women to tell them that they are not or to even attempt to save them. The quest for international/cross-cultural women coalitions, then, is not about White women's appropriation of the gender, sexual, queer, racial, ethnic, and disability struggles of minority women. Rather, the quest for an international/cross-cultural women's coalition should be about making White women better participant observers who may speak at times but may also remain reserved—not through ignorance but through experience, in the face of sexual and gender oppression directed at minority women.

NOTES

1. Judith Surkis, "Ethics and Violence: Simone de Beauvoir, Djamila Boupacha, and the Algerian War," *French Politics, Culture & Society* 28, no. 2 (2010): 44.

2. Gisèle Halimi, *Milk for the Orange Tree* (London: Quartet Books, 1990), 300–1.

3. Ibid.

4. Karen L. Shelby, "Intersubjectivity, Politics, Violence: Simone de Beauvoir and Colonialism" (Chicago' American Political Science Association Paper, September 2–September 5, 2004), 5.

5. Beauvoir, "Pour Djamila Boupacha," 1.

6. Halimi, *Milk for the Orange Tree*, 297.

7. Gisèle Halimi, "D'Henri Alleg à Djamila Boupacha," *Les Temps Modernes* 15, no. 171 (June 1960): 1822–27.

8. Beauvoir, *Djamila Boupacha.*

9. Simone de Beauvoir adopted the nickname "The Beaver" among her close acquaintances. Because she was such a hardworker!

10. Halimi, *Milk for the Orange Tree*, 298, 300–1.

11. Shannon Sullivan, "Whiteness as Wise Provincialism: Royce and the Rehabilitation of a Racial Category," *Transactions of the Charles S. Peirce Society: A Quarterly Journal in American Philosophy* 44, no. 2 (2008): 252.

12. Julien S. Murphy, "Introduction," in *Political Writings* (Chicago, IL: University of Illinois Press, 2012), 265.

13. Ibid.

14. Sartre, *Colonialism and Neocolonialism*, 36.

15. Sullivan, "Whiteness as Wise Provincialism," 252.

16. Kruks, "Beauvoir," 103–4.

17. Ursula Tidd, "The Self-Other Relation in Beauvoir's Ethics and Autobiography," *Hypatia* 14, no. 4 (Autumn 1999): 171.

18. Toril Moi, "Meaning What We Say," in *The Legacy of Simone de Beauvoir* (Oxford: Oxford University Press, 2004), 146.

19. Homi Bhabha, "Introduction," *French Politics, Culture & Society* 28, no. 2 (2010): 1.

20. Ibid.

21. Ibid.

22. Halimi, *Milk for the Orange Tree*, 298.

23. Ibid.

24. Ibid.

25. Ibid., 299.

26. Bonnie Mann, *Sovereign Masculinity: Gender Lessons from the War on Terror*, Studies in Feminist Philosophy (New York, NY: Oxford University Press, 2014), 22.

27. Lila Abu-Lughod, "Do Muslim Women Really Need Saving? Anthropological Reflections on Cultural Relativism and Its Others," *American Anthropologist*, New Series, 104, no. 3 (2002): 783–90.

28. Kimberly Hutchings, "Simone de Beauvoir and the Ambiguous Ethics of Political Violence," *Hypatia* 22, no. 3 (2007): 113.

29. Laura Bush, "George W. Bush: Radio Address by Mrs. Bush," November 17, 2001, 1. http://www.presidency.ucsb.edu/ws/?pid=24992

30. Ibid.

Part IV

CONCLUSION

Chapter 6

Toward an Inclusive
Beauvoirian Scholarship

In this book, in order to present the position of Beauvoir as a *colonizer* in the French colonial complex, I have focused on four topics within contemporary philosophical inquiry, each in separate chapters, all covering to different degrees the colonial themes of freedom, identity, and violence. The topics evidence Beauvoir's blindness to race and gender *intersectionality,* as apparent in her liaison with Djamila Boupacha and her analysis on the Black slave in *The Second Sex.* This blindness affected how Beauvoir thought about the situations and struggles of colonized women.

The other three topics point to her concern with the use and value of violence in post–World War France, in terms of the French versus the colonized Other; *The Second Sex's* testimony of White women as "The Other" (and comparing those who experience class, slavery, and racial oppression to the history of the colonized); and her commitment to an *inter-subjective ethics.* To conclude, I will not review my main argument—which shows that, at least some of the time, there cannot be discussions on French colonialism without taking into account the roles of women, White or non-White, within that system, as it has in part been reflected in the work of Beauvoir—which is based much more on questions of method within the development of French philosophy, feminism, critical race philosophy, and postcolonial philosophy. Instead, I turn to a passage in Toril Moi's book *Simone de Beauvoir: The Making of an Intellectual Woman* to show the perpetual trend among Beauvoir scholars to raise the question of race only when it alludes to problems relating to the situation of White women, a type of analysis, I would argue, that further negates the situation of women of color who are faced with not only a gender/sex problem but also a race problem.

Moi claims the following, "Neglected by dominant political discourses, the subject of women's oppression was, if anything, even more marginal in

France than questions of colonialism and racism. It is not a coincidence that throughout her essay [*The Second Sex*] Beauvoir makes frequent comparisons between the situation of women and that of Jews and blacks. As we shall see, there is much to be gained by relating her political analysis to that of Frantz Fanon, whose *Black Skin,/White Masks* was published in Paris in 1952, only three years after *The Second Sex*."[1] Moi posits here that, in 1940s and 1950s France, the French were more concerned about colonialism and racism than questions of gender and sex as featured in *The Second Sex*. I argue that Moi's perspective on the reception of gender and sexual topics in post–World War France fails to take into account the gender, sexual, and political movements led by the French feminist suffragettes who set the stage for the reception of Beauvoir's book in the late 1940s. In France, the suffragettes did not just work on the right to vote, they were also concerned with the regulation of prostitution, fair wages for women, the right to divorce for women, and gender equality for women in general. To me, the topics raised by the first-wave feminists set the stage for the reception of Beauvoir's book, which could be considered a work of second-wave feminism and that was surfacing in an environment already fraught with prejudices against women's oppression. The goal of my analysis is not to oppose Moi on climate of gender and sex versus attitudes toward colonialism and racism in France. Instead, I want to show that while the French public was already familiar with the conflicts surrounding the rights of women with regard to their sex and gender, the marginality to this subject was no different than the marginality of subjects related to the situation and rights of the colonized. I also want to show that comparisons between gender and sex and race tend to systematically dismiss the position of minority women who faced both gender/sex and race problems that they cannot always tease apart.

Of course, Moi urges other contemporary feminist scholars to relate the analysis of Beauvoir to Fanon. However, the reasons she does so are different than my enterprise in this book. When using Fanon in feminist discourse, Moi wants us to compare race to gender/sex—not to consider the intersectionality of race and gender/sex. In this book, I have compared the analysis of Fanon to Beauvoir only with regard to their views on violence. To claim that comparing a minority author to a White author is possible when we want to present a written intervention of race to dominant discourses is problematic. To claim that comparing a minority author to a White author is also possible when to we want to compare the relationship between race and gender/sex is problematic. Furthermore, as she urges us to compare Fanon to Beauvoir, Moi seems to implicitly relate the problem of race to the situation of the Black man and the problem of gender/sex to the situation of the White woman. Kathryn Gines, since her article on Beauvoir was published in *Convergences: Black Feminism and Continental Philosophy*, in 2010, has written and presented on this issue to a fault in order to urge Beauvoir scholars to stay away from the problem of the race/gender analogy that can be read into in Beauvoir's works beginning with *The Second Sex*. Here as well, in the conclusion of my book, I follow Gines's analysis, as Penelope Deutscher has remarked in "Symposia on Gender, Race and Philosophy,"[2] and call upon Beauvoir scholars to renounce their concerns for the race/gender analogy in favor of an intersectional analysis that not only already accept the position of White women and Black men, but also more fundamentally accept the position of minority women.

Rather than writing women of color out of postcolonial feminist philosophy, we ought to find better and more innovative ways to include them in this branch of philosophy. Doing so would not only be inclusive but also enable us to better gauge the participation of White men and women and, men of color in postcolonial discourses. This book is not just an intervention in the scholarship on Beauvoir. It is also meant to give a voice to women of color, such as Paulette Nardal, in postcolonial feminist philosophy. As Beauvoir extended the baton to Djamila Boupacha and Gisele Halimi, I extend the baton to Beauvoir's scholars, White or not, so that they can think about including minority women (including ourselves) in publications and conference presentations as I have attempted to do here by re-writing the history of Beauvoir as a French *colonizer* woman who not only fought against the colonial system but was also compromised by it.

A recent development of this type of research can be seen in Stephanie Rivera Berruz's article "At the Crossroads: Latina Identity and Simone de Beauvoir's *The Second Sex*," published in 2016 in *Hypatia*. Berruz presents an unconventional approach to *The Second Sex*, arguing that the book falls short of being able to account for the multidimensionality of identity—such as Latina identity—insofar as Beauvoir's argument rests upon the comparison between racial and gendered oppression that is understood through the Black-White binary.[3] In other words, Berruz claims that certain dominant discourses on race, such as those based on the Black-White binary, when associated with the question of gender, as Beauvoir does in *The Second Sex*, can undermine the representation of women of mixed heritage in feminist philosophy. Berruz also argues that Beauvoir, in taking race to denote enslavement as comparable to the situation of White women, supports the central claims of the alterity of White women thereby participating in the all-too-easy appropriation of Black suffering for a philosophical discussion on White women.[4] According to Berruz's analysis not only can Beauvoir's analysis on gender exploit the oppression of Blacks but it also allows for mixed-race identities to fall through the cracks.[5] The analysis of Beauvoir re-inscribes the philosophy of racial purity, which is highly problematic when trying to understand not just Latina identity in the contemporary world but also the legacy of mixed race and/or mulatto slaves in places such as Haiti, Brazil, Dominican Republic, or the United States. Moreover, because Berruz's criticism of Beauvoir's studies is based on Latina identity, which is a form of colonial identity, Berruz's criticism also serves to underline the colonial trend in contemporary Beauvoir's studies. In the end, I support the type of analysis presented by Berruz because it opens the borders of White feminist philosophy to include women at the margins and signals the shortcomings and progress of studies of the essays of Simone de Beauvoir.

Finally, in the article "What Should White People do?" Linda Alcoff echoes the kind of criticism that goes against the trend of White feminism represented by Toril Moi. In appealing to Fanon, Moi suggests that Fanon's work cannot be attempted by Beauvoir or even Moi herself. Like Alcoff, I question Moi's revelation about the problems and complexity of White identity,[6] from which Moi seems to suggest that an intersubjective and intersectional discourse (from either her perspective or Beauvoir's subject position) is almost nearly impossible. Yet, as it is with the analysis this book presents, in staging parts of the history of imperial and/or colonial France through the reflections of Beauvoir, I am putting into question the relation of White women to whiteness, White supremacy, and White privilege, and am therefore asking what the role of White identity is to certain discourses on race. Furthermore, like Alcoff, who asks "What is White women's relation to whiteness?" I am asking "What is Beauvoir and her White female predecessors to Whiteness?" They are part of both the problem *and* the solution of our racist world, and must assume their White identity to address racialized gender conflicts, as, for example, Fanon and Paulette Nardal attempted to do. If Moi needs to incorporate the philosophy of Fanon to the work of Beauvoir as the analysis relates to the problem of racism, then that is a problem because Moi can take up this opportunity developed through her own analysis to discuss in more intersubjective and intersectional ways the issues connecting gendered racial discrimination to White supremacy. This book has been written as a result of my Black female multicultural identity. It resembles Berruz's analysis but can also invite Moi to give an account of her racialized gender identity, which in turn can address both the problems raised by the work of Fanon and Beauvoir, problems that Moi's analysis seems to be concerned about. It is not just up to Blacks or Latinas to address the problem of race; Whites can also use their subject position to address the race problem we all share.

Our interests in Beauvoir's legacy has to stop, in Mariana Ortega's word, "being lovingly, knowingly ignorant,"[7] a state of critical consciousness that I would add is based on unintentional biases or racism and sexism that further divide White feminism from the worlds of women of color. This divide is based on White women who have understood the need for a better way to perceive women of color but who continue to arrogantly perceive the situation of women of color, to distort their objects of perception, all while thinking that they are loving perceivers—or knowing perceivers—who care about the diversity of not just ideas but also experiences.[8] Following Ortega's criticism, it is important to see that for women of color, doing feminism is about ending racism, not simply about engaging in a theoretical debate.[9] It is with this type of imperative, in my case, the imperative of using feminism in an attempt to end racism by developing more gender inclusive narratives on the last stage of French colonialism, that I have written this book. Any kind of well-performed feminist interventions into the way we theorize about the intersectionality and intersubjectivity of racism to sexism within our intellectual philosophical history can participate in reassessing racism because these types of feminist interventions contribute to the development of an anti-racist world—free of racism, sexism, and classism. Utilizing our standpoint to access the legacy of a racist political system, such as French colonialism, can enable us to understand why there is a need for philosophical and feminist anti-racist discourses.

NOTES

1. Toril Moi, *Simone de Beauvoir: The Making of an Intellectual Woman*, 2nd ed. (Oxford; New York, NY: Oxford University Press, 2008), 209.

2. Penelope Deutscher, "Symposia on Gender, Race and Philosophy," 12, no. 1 (Spring 2016): 1–6. http://sgrp.typepad.com/sgrp/

3. Stephanie Rivera Berruz, "At the Crossroads: Latina Identity and Simone de Beauvoir's The Second Sex," *Hypatia* 31, no. 2 (May 2016): 319.

4. Ibid., 331.

5. Ibid., 330.

6. Linda Martín Alcoff, "What Should White People Do?" *Hypatia* 13, no. 3 (1998): 7.

7. Mariana Ortega, "Being Lovingly, Knowingly Ignorant: White Feminism and Women of Color," *Hypatia* 21, no. 3 (2006): 56.

8. Ibid., 60.

9. Ibid., 68.

Bibliography

Abu-Lughod, Lila. "Do Muslim Women Really Need Saving? Anthropological Reflections on Cultural Relativism and Its Others." *American Anthropologist*, New Series, 104, no. 3 (2002): 783–90.

Alcoff, Linda Martín. "What Should White People Do?" *Hypatia* 13, no. 3 (1998): 6–26.

Aldrich, Robert. *France's Overseas Frontier: Départements et Territoires D'outre-Mer.* New York, NY: Cambridge University Press, 1992.

Amos, Valerie and Pratibha Parmar. "Challenging Imperial Feminism." *Feminist Review* 1, no. 80 (January 1, 2005): 44–63.

Arendt, Hannah. *On Violence.* New York, NY: Harcourt, 1970.

Arp, Kristana. *The Bonds of Freedom: Simone de Beauvoir's Existentialist Ethics.* Berkeley, CA: Open Court, 2001.

Bauer, Nancy. *Simone de Beauvoir, Philosophy, and Feminism.* New York, NY: Columbia University Press, 2001.

Beauvoir, Simone de. *Djamila Boupacha.* New York, NY: Macmillan, 1962.

———. *The Ethics of Ambiguity.* Secaucus, NJ: The Citadel Press, 1972.

———. *Force of Circumstance, Vol. 1, After the War, 1944–1952.* [S.l.]: Marlowe & Co, n.d.

———. *Force of Circumstance, Vol. 2: Hard Times, 1952–1962.* New York, NY: Paragon House, 1992.

———. *The Mandarins.* New York, NY: W. W. Norton & Company, 1999.

———. *Philosophical Writings.* Urbana, IL: University of Illinois Press, 2004.

———. "Pour Djamila Boupacha." *Le Monde* (1960): 5.

———. *The Second Sex.* New York, NY: Vintage Books, 1989.

Bergoffen, Debra. *Introduction to Philosophical Writings by Simone de Beauvoir.* Chicago, IL: University of Illinois Press, 2004, 79–87.

Bernasconi, Robert. *How to Read Sartre.* London: Granta, 2006.

Berruz, Stephanie Rivera. "At the Crossroads: Latina Identity and Simone de Beauvoir's The Second Sex." *Hypatia* 31, no. 2 (May 2016): 319–33.

Bhabha, Homi. "Introduction." *French Politics, Culture & Society* 28, no. 2 (2010): 1–3.

Burton, Richard. *French and West Indian: Martinique, Guadeloupe, and French Guiana Today.* Charlottesville, VA: University Press of Virginia, 1995.

Bush, Laura. "George W. Bush: Radio Address by Mrs. Bush." November 17, 2001. http://www.presidency.ucsb.edu/ws/?pid=24992

Caputi, Mary. "Beauvoir and the Case of Djamila Boupacha." In *Simone de Beauvoir's Political Thinking*, edited by Lori Jo Marso and Patricia Moynagh. Chicago, IL: University of Illinois Press, 2006.

Cesaire, Aime. *Discourse on Colonialism.* New York, NY: Monthly Review Press, 2000.

Deutscher, Penelope. "Symposia on Gender, Race and Philosophy." 1, no. Spring (2016). http://sgrp.typepad.com/sgrp/

Fairchild, Halford H. "Frantz Fanon's *The Wretched of the Earth* in Contemporary Perspective." *Journal of Black Studies* 25, no. 2 (December 1, 1994): 191–99.

Fallaize, Elizabeth. *Simone de Beauvoir: A Critical Reader.* London: Routledge, 1998.

Fanon, Frantz. *Black Skin, White Masks.* New York, NY: Grove Press, 1967.

———. "De La Violence." *Les Temps Modernes* 16, no. 181 (May 1961): 1453–93.

———. *The Wretched of the Earth.* Translated by Richard Philcox. Introduction by Jean-Paul Sartre and Homi K. Bhabha. New York, NY: Grove Press, 2004.

Gendzier, Irene L. "Frantz Fanon: In Search of Justice." *Middle East Journal* 20, no. 4 (October 1, 1966): 534–44.

Ghosh, Jayati. "Simone de Beauvoir: In Search of Freedom and Honesty." *Social Scientist* 14, no. 4 (April 1, 1986): 64–66. https://doi.org/10.2307/3517182

Gibson, Nigel. *Frantz Fanon: The Postcolonial Imagination.* Malden, MA: Polity Press, 2003.

———. *Living Fanon: Global Perspectives.* Contemporary Black History. New York, NY: Palgrave Macmillan, 2011.

Gines, Kathryn T. "Arendt Violence/Power Distinction and Sartre's Violence/Counter-Violence Distinction: The Phenomenology of Violence in Colonial and Post-Colonial Contexts." In *Phenomenologies of Violence.* Boston, MA: Brill, 2014.

———. "Comparative and Competing Frameworks of Oppression in Simone de Beauvoir's The Second Sex." *Graduate Faculty Philosophy Journal* 35, no. 1–2 (2014): 251–73.

———. "Sartre, Beauvoir, and the Race/Gender Analogy." In *Convergences: Black Feminism and Continental Philosophy*, edited by Maria del Guadalupe Davidson, Kathryn T. Gines, and Donna-Dale L. Marcano. New York, NY: SUNY Press, 2010, 35–52.

Gregory, Abigail. *Women in Contemporary France.* New York, NY: Berg, 2000.

Halimi, Gisèle. "D'Henri Alleg À Djamila Boupacha." *Les Temps Modernes* 15, no. 171 (June 1960): 1822–32.

———. *Milk for the Orange Tree.* London: Quartet Books, 1990.

Hirschmann, N. J. *Gender, Class, and Freedom in Modern Political Theory.* Princeton, NJ: Princeton University Press, 2008.

Hourdin, Georges. *Simone de Beauvoir et La Liberté. Tout Le Monde En Parle.* Paris: Les Éditions du Cerf, c1962.

Hutchings, Kimberly. "Simone de Beauvoir and the Ambiguous Ethics of Political Violence." *Hypatia* 22, no. 3 (2007): 111–32.

Jinadu, L. Adele. "Fanon: The Revolutionary as Social Philosopher." *The Review of Politics* 34, no. 3 (July 1, 1972): 433–36.

Kirkland, Emily and McTighe Musil. *La Marianne Noire*. Los Angeles, CA: University of California, Los Angeles, 2007.

Kruks, Sonia. "Beauvoir: The Weight of Situation." In *Simone de Beauvoir: A Critical Reader*. New York, NY: Routledge, 1998, 43–72.

———. *Simone de Beauvoir and the Politics of Ambiguity*. Studies in Feminist Philosophy. New York, NY: Oxford University Press, 2012.

———. "Simone de Beauvoir and the Politics of Privilege." *Hypatia* 20, no. 1 (2005): 178–205.

Locke, John. *Second Treatise of Government*. Indianapolis, IN: Hackett Pub. Co., 1980.

Macey, David. *Frantz Fanon: A Life*. London: Granta Books, 2000.

———. "Frantz Fanon, or the Difficulty of Being Martinican." *History Workshop Journal* 58 (October 1, 2004): 211–23.

Mann, Bonnie. *Sovereign Masculinity: Gender Lessons from the War on Terror*. Studies in Feminist Philosophy. New York, NY: Oxford University Press, 2014.

Mbembe, Achille. *Critique of Black Reason*. Translated by Laurent Dubois. Durham, NC: Duke University Press Books, 2017.

Moi, Toril. "Meaning What We Say." In *The Legacy of Simone de Beauvoir*. Oxford: Oxford University Press, 2004, 139–60.

———. *Simone de Beauvoir: The Making of an Intellectual Woman*. 2nd ed. New York, NY: Oxford University Press, 2008.

Murphy, Ann V. "Between Generosity and Violence: Toward a Revolutionary Politics in the Philosophy of Simone de Beauvoir." In *The Philosophy of Simone de Beauvoir: Critical Essays*, edited by Margaret A. Simons. Indianapolis, IN: Indiana University Press, 2006, 262–75.

Murphy, Julien S. "Beauvoir and the Algerian War: Toward a Postcolonial Ethics." In *Feminist Interpretations of Simone de Beauvoir*. University Park, PA: Penn State University Press, 1995, 263–97.

———. "Introduction." In *Political Writings*. Chicago, IL: University of Illinois Press, 2012, 261–65.

Nardal, Paulette. *Beyond Negritude: Essays from Woman in the City*. Albany, NY: SUNY Press, 2009.

Ortega, Mariana. "Being Lovingly, Knowingly Ignorant: White Feminism and Women of Color." *Hypatia* 21, no. 3, 2006, 56–74.

Pateman, Carole. *The Sexual Contract*. Stanford, CA: Stanford University Press, 1988.

Quellel, Charif. "Franz Fanon and Colonized Man." *Africa Today* 17, no. 1 (January 1, 1970): 8–11.

Rabaka, Reiland. *Forms of Fanonism: Frantz Fanon's Critical Theory and the Dialectics of Decolonization*. Lanham, MD: Lexington Books, 2010.

Sanos, Sandrine. *Simone de Beauvoir: Creating a Feminist Existence in the World*. New York, NY: Oxford University Press, 2016.

Sartre, Jean-Paul. *Colonialism and Neocolonialism.* New York, NY: Routledge, 2006.

———. *Life Situations: Essays Written and Spoken.* New York, NY: Pantheon Books, 1977.

Sharpley-Whiting, T. *Frantz Fanon: Conflicts and Feminisms.* Lanham, MD: Rowman & Littlefield, 1998.

Shelby, Karen L. *Intersubjectivity, Politics, Violence: Simone de Beauvoir and Colonialism.* Chicago, IL: American Political Science Association Paper, September 2–September 5, 2004.

Simons, Margaret. *Beauvoir and The Second Sex: Feminism, Race, and the Origins of Existentialism.* Lanham, MD: Rowman & Littlefield Publishers, 1999.

———. *Feminist Interpretations of Simone de Beauvoir.* University Park, PA: Pennsylvania State University Press, 1995.

———. *The Philosophy of Simone de Beauvoir: Critical Essays.* Bloomington, IN: Indiana University Press, 2006.

Sullivan, Shannon. "Whiteness as Wise Provincialism: Royce and the Rehabilitation of a Racial Category." *Transactions of the Charles S. Peirce Society: A Quarterly Journal in American Philosophy* 44, no. 2 (2008): 236–62.

Surkis, Judith. "Ethics and Violence: Simone de Beauvoir, Djamila Boupacha, and the Algerian War." *French Politics, Culture & Society* 28, no. 2 (2010), 38–55.

Tidd, Ursula. "The Self-Other Relation in Beauvoir's Ethics and Autobiography." *Hypatia* 14, no. 4 (Autumn 1999): 163–74.

———. *Simone De Beauvoir.* London: Reaktion Books, 2009.

Vintges, Karen. *A New Dawn for the Second Sex: Women's Freedom Practices in World Perspective.* Amsterdam: Amsterdam University Press, 2017.

———. *Philosophy as Passion: The Thinking of Simone de Beauvoir.* Bloomington, IN: Indiana University Press, 1996.

Ward, Julie K. and Tommy L. Lott. *Philosophers on Race: Critical Essays.* Malden, MA: Blackwell, 2002.

Wehrs, Donald R. "Sartre's Legacy in Postcolonial Theory; Or, Who's Afraid of Non-Western Historiography and Cultural Studies?" *New Literary History* 34, no. 4 (October 1, 2003): 761–89.

West, Traci C. "Extending Black Feminist Sisterhood in the Face of Violence." In *Convergences: Black Feminism and Continental Philosophy.* Albany, NY: SUNY Press, 2010, 157–82.

Winegarten, Renee. *Simone de Beauvoir: A Critical View.* Berg Women's Series. New York, NY: St. Martin's Press, 1988.

Zack, Naomi. *Thinking about Race.* Belmont, CA: Thomson Wadsworth, 2006.

Index

About the Author

Nathalie Nya currently teaches in the Department of Philosophy at John Carroll University, Cleveland, Ohio. She holds a PhD degree in Philosophy from Pennsylvania State University and a master's degree in Philosophy from the University of California. Her fields of expertise include Social and Political Philosophy, Ethics, Social Justice, Feminist Philosophy and Critical Race Philosophy, and her research primarily focuses on the intersection of class, race, and gender in Africana Philosophy and twentieth century European Philosophy.